George Washington • John Adams • Thomas Jefferson • James Madison • James Monroe • John Quincy Adams • Andrew Jackson • Martin Van Buren • William Henry Harrison • John Tyler • James K. Polk • Zachary Taylor • Millard Fillmore • Franklin Pierce • James Buchanan • Abraham Lincoln • Andrew Johnson • Ulysses S. Grant • Rutherford B. Hayes • James A. Garfield • Chester A. Arthur • Grover Cleveland • Benjamin Harrison • Grover Cleveland • William McKinley • Theodore Roosevelt • William H. Taft • Woodrow Wilson • Warren G. Harding • Calvin Coolidge • Herbert C. Hoover • Franklin D. Roosevelt • Harry S Truman • Dwight D. Eisenhower • John F. Kennedy • Lyndon B. Johnson • Richard M. Nixon • Gerald R. Ford • James Earl Carter • Ronald Reagan • George Bush • William Jefferson Clinton

Table of Contents

George Washington • John Adams • Thomas Jefferson • James Madison • James Monroe • John Quincy Adams • Andrew Jackson • Martin Van Buren • William Henry Harrison • John Tyler • James K. Polk • Zachary Taylor • Millard Fillmore • Franklin Pierce • James Buchanan • Abraham Lincoln • Andrew Johnson • Ulysses S. Grant • Rutherford B. Hayes • James A. Garfield • Chester A. Arthur • Grover Cleveland • Benjamin Harrison • Grover Cleveland • William McKinley • Theodore Roosevelt • William H. Taft • Woodrow Wilson • Warren G. Harding • Calvin Coolidge • Herbert C. Hoover • Franklin D. Roosevelt • Harry S Truman • Dwight D. Eisenhower • John F. Kennedy • Lyndon B. Johnson • Richard M. Nixon • Gerald R. Ford • James Earl Carter • Ronald Reagan • George Bush • William Jefferson Clinton

Plays About the Presidents

**Short Classroom Plays,
Background Information,
and Activities about
12 Influential Presidents**

by Timothy Nolan

S C H O L A S T I C
PROFESSIONAL BOOKS

NEW YORK · TORONTO · LONDON · AUCKLAND · SYDNEY

Like all my work, this book is dedicated to my wonderful
wife, Susannah. It is also dedicated to the memory of
Mr. George Maloney, a wonderful teacher and great
man, who taught me to love the history of our country
and the people who have created it. Thanks, Mr. M.

Introduction

The Story in History

Imagine for a moment that your life and the lives of each of your students were reduced to the following set of facts and numbers:

☆ Name

☆ Date of birth

☆ One significant accomplishment

☆ Date of death (if applicable)

Important, of course, but not nearly a complete picture. There is so much more that goes into a life—influences, beliefs, fears, hopes, loves, goals. And yet those are the very things that are frequently forgotten when we examine historical figures. Too often the focus is on the "four facts," and when students are asked what they know about a particular president or historical figure, they have only a few general facts to recite.

In many ways, the dramatic form is the perfect medium for bringing out the story in history. While we cannot reproduce exact dialogue or fully re-create historical events, drama does allow you, your students, and other observers to see the development of historical figures—what led up to their moment of destiny, and how their experiences shaped their lives.

The story of the United States is vital to the educational experience of young people because it is true and because it is part of a direct line that leads straight to them as Americans. It is also a story as fascinating and absorbing as any in literature. By presenting it in a cross-curricular context, we hope that it will increase students' fascination for the variety of influences that contribute to our national characters.

Our 42 (as of this writing) presidents have been national leaders, national symbols, and have sometimes shaped an era. In many ways, they reflected as well as shaped the customs and mores of the times they lived in and served. By presenting particular episodes of their lives, it is our hope that these leaders, who are so often idealized due to their historical significance, will be seen more fully as human beings.

Our Purpose

These plays are intended to enhance students' appreciation and knowledge of our American heritage, and to:

☆ build literacy;

☆ increase class involvement;

☆ encourage appreciation for theater and acting;

☆ inspire independent writing;

☆ involve at-risk or withdrawn students.

Reading plays aloud is one of the most effective ways to promote literacy and history in your classroom. We encourage you to invite students to perform these plays as part of your reading, language arts, or social studies curriculum.

How to Use this Book

Casting Every effort has been made to have many characters in each play, including important characters for both boys and girls. However, don't feel limited by traditional roles. It can become an inclusive activity that helps to forge the connection between students and their heritage to experiment with nontraditional casting of ethnicities and genders.

Preparation and Predicting Before you begin, you might suggest students spend a few moments acquainting themselves with the characters they are playing by reading over the lines. It will enhance the educational experience, not to mention understanding and enjoyment, if you use a prediction exercise before the dramatic reading. Ask students if they have ever heard of the president in the play and what they know about him. Do they know anything about his background, his family, his life? Try using one of the classroom activities as a predicting activity, or have a volunteer look up and read aloud materials about the president's life and times.

Each play is followed by a brief biography that can be used as a jumping-off point for predicting and preparation activities.

A great predicting activity is to have each student, the night before reading the play in class, find one fact about the president's life. Then have them each bring their facts into class for discussion. This will give students something to listen for (prediction and confirmation) as they read the play.

Classroom Activities

At the end of each play are classroom activities, divided into three categories: "talk about it" for classroom discussion, "write about it" for written reports or small group projects, and "report on it" for group or class projects of larger scope. The activities focus on one or more themes of the play (bravery in "In Memory of Joe: John F. Kennedy," acting on personal belief versus the common good in "The Deal of the Century: Thomas Jefferson"). The activities are meant to be used in conjunction with the plays, but by no means should you limit your discussion or lesson to what is presented. Rather, consider using this material as a means to an end.

Many of the activities involve presenting reports to the class. As one of our purposes is to promote literacy, especially oral literacy, encourage students to present their reports to the class whenever possible, and have the class ask questions. You should find that asking every student to take a chance making a presentation will foster an atmosphere of mutual respect. The more you do this, the more comfortable your students will become speaking before a group, and the greater the pride they will take in their work.

You can move the activities one step further by having the students write their own dramas. Try having them treat the same episode from different points of view (other characters, etc.), or have them put their new knowledge to work by writing "next day" plays—pieces that continue the story.

Many activities are reenactments or role-playing games. Try assigning students different historical roles, have them research their roles so they know who they are playing, and then do historical reenactments in class. Rather than relying on lines and scripts, students may use their research and recall to improvise their roles. They will not only learn research and recall skills, but will develop confidence in learning and in themselves. They will also feel closer to the historical figures.

Larger Performances As a way of encouraging and nurturing students' enthusiasm, think about other ways to perform the plays. For example, try assigning plays of the same historical era to groups of students and let them rehearse and perform the dramas. You could also organize a "play day" around an era or other theme (the Civil War, the Great Depression, the two Roosevelts, influences of first ladies, Civil Rights, and so on).

If you find the class is hungry to perform the plays for a wider audience, take the plays before the whole school. Try calling on parents to become involved by donating or making costumes, building sets, making posters and doing other publicity. You will find that these activities can be done cheaply and with out much trouble—students can paint sets on large poster paper, which can then be hung at the back of the stage; Mom or Grandma's old dress could become a period costume. This can be a great way to celebrate Women's History Month, Black History Month, or, best of all, President's Week.

We hope you enjoy these stories of the presidents.

George Washington
A Christmastime Victory

CAST

NARRATOR ONE

NARRATOR TWO

GENERAL NATHANIEL GREENE

GEORGE WASHINGTON

GENERAL JOHN SULLIVAN

MARTHA CUSTIS, JR.

MARTHA WASHINGTON

JOHN CUSTIS

CONTINENTAL SOLDIERS
  (JACK, TOM, FREDERICK, PAUL)

★ Scene One

NARRATOR ONE: Welcome to the Continental Army camp along the Delaware River in Pennsylvania. It is December 1776. It has been five months since the Continental Congress, located in Philadelphia, Pennsylvania, declared the independence of the American colonies, and the Revolutionary War is raging on.

NARRATOR TWO: At this point, it is not going well for the new Americans. As General George Washington meets with his staff—Generals Nathaniel Greene and John Sullivan—they give him the news.

GREENE: Sir, things look bad. We lost a thousand men at the Battle of Long Island, along with their weapons and supplies. As for the men we have left, their enlistments are ended, and we have no money to pay them. Without money, they certainly will not reenlist. So it looks like our great revolution is doomed to failure.

GEORGE: What do you mean, we don't have the money to pay the soldiers or buy the supplies? Congress was supposed to send it to us!

SULLIVAN: *(looking sheepish and shrugging)* I know they were supposed to send it, sir. And I hoped that being in Pennsylvania near their headquarters, we would hear from them faster...but...

GREENE: *(interrupting, nervously)* But when Congress heard that we were coming into Pennsylvania, they feared the Redcoats would follow us, and...and...they have fled the city!

GEORGE: Blast! How can this be? The Congress declares war, then expects us to fight it without weapons, ammunition, food for the men, blankets to keep them warm, or money to pay them what they are worth. This meeting is over, gentlemen. That's all.

NARRATOR ONE: Outside the meeting, the generals spoke of their worries about their commander.

SULLIVAN: General Washington seems to be desperate.

GREENE: Well, our situation is desperate. Can you imagine what the British will do to us if we lose this war? The colonies will be back under King George's rule, and we'll be hanged as traitors! If only we could get what we need from the Congress, we could mount an attack on the British.

SULLIVAN: If only.

★ Scene Two

NARRATOR TWO: Meanwhile, at Mount Vernon, Martha Washington was also worried. She had received George's letters and knew how close he was to giving up hope. The Washington children, John and Martha Custis, Jr., loved him, and they were as worried as Martha.

MARTHA, JR.: Why does Daddy need money, Mama? Can't the soldiers just fight?

MARTHA: With what, dear? Their bare hands? And on empty stomachs, in the freezing cold? And against the British, who are so well armed and well fed?

JOHN: Well, can't our men just sit tight until help comes?

MARTHA: What if help doesn't come? And your daddy says every day he worries about the large Redcoat army getting closer. If they were to attack our men now, all would be lost.

MARTHA, JR.: How did this happen? I thought the army was doing so well!

MARTHA: They did well in New England in the early parts of the war, then the army moved down to New York. They fortified Manhattan and Brooklyn with soldiers, but he didn't think the British were going to come up into Staten Island. The British came at our army from the back, and our men were trapped.

MARTHA, JR.: I remember.

MARTHA: Daddy managed to get what was left of the army out of New York, across New Jersey and into Pennsylvania, but now the British are following him. Our men are safe for the moment, but they are running out of food and supplies.

JOHN: So if they can't get food and supplies from the Congress, can they get them from somewhere else?

MARTHA: I don't know, son. But I have faith in your father. I'm sure he'll think of something.

★ Scene Three

NARRATOR ONE: Jack, a Continental soldier, enters George's tent.

JACK: General, one of our scouts has made it back to camp. He reports that there is a band of Hessian mercenaries from the British army encamped at Trenton.

SULLIVAN: That's right across the Delaware River from our camp!

GEORGE: Let's have the report.

JACK: Well, sir, according to the scout, there are over one thousand. It looks like they're going to be there for a while.

GEORGE: We have twenty-four hundred men here, so they can't have come to attack us. I'd like to know just why they are here now, though …

JACK: It seemed like they came to hold the camp until the British arrive.

GEORGE: Maybe…General Greene, what date is it?

GREENE: December twentieth, sir.

SULLIVAN: I meant to speak with you on that subject, sir. The men are asking if they could return home for Christmas.

GEORGE: Christmas—that's it! The Hessians are camping there because it's Christmas! Of course! They're not here to attack us—they don't even know we're here—they've simply set up a camp in order to take a Christmas leave. Sullivan?

SULLIVAN: Yes, sir!

GEORGE: Cancel all Christmas leave for our men.

SULLIVAN: General, you are aware that the morale of the troops is very low.

GEORGE: I know. I know that they want to go home. *(Smiling and clapping his hands together.)* But maybe we can give them something better than a leave.

GREENE: I don't understand, sir.

GEORGE: You will, Greene, you will. You all will. Leave me a moment to think, all of you. Dismissed.

GREENE, SULLIVAN, and JACK: Yes, sir!

★ Scene Four

NARRATOR TWO: Jack went back to his tent, where other Continentals, Frederick, Tom, and Paul, gathered around him.

PAUL: Did you tell the general we're hungry and cold?

JACK: Believe me, General Washington knows what we need.

FREDERICK: So what's he going to do?

JACK: He's got a plan, a big plan, I can tell.

FREDERICK: How can you tell?

JACK: Because I saw his face when I told him about the Hessians. I could tell he was thinking of something, something big, something he wouldn't even tell his other generals!

TOM: Gee, what do you think it could be?

PAUL: Whatever it is, I hope it includes food and blankets.

★ Scene Five

NARRATOR ONE: George was in his tent, thinking of a daring plan, and when he was sure it would work, he called his generals together to inform them.

GEORGE: Gentlemen, the Hessians across the river are rich in supplies, food, blankets, and ammunition. And they are lying over there, resting through the Christmas holidays. They don't expect an attack. We can load up in rowboats, move silently across the Delaware River under cover of night, and be upon the Hessians by dawn. We will catch them completely by surprise.

GREENE: Rowboats? We'll need hundreds.

GEORGE: We will use and reuse the boats we have until all our men are across the river. It will take all night, but with ten men in ten boats each, we'll have to make twenty trips. The river is not wide at this point. We will all be across just before dawn breaks.

SULLIVAN: But sir, the river is choked with ice!

GEORGE: It will be dark, and with the Hessians celebrating, we will be able to take our time. We'll take all night, if we need to. And once we're all across, we'll surround the Hessian camp and spring on them at first light! Any other questions?

SULLIVAN: Attacking on Christmas, is that…fair?

GEORGE: Look here—our men are freezing to death. We are about to run out of food. And, worst of all, their spirit is suffering. We have not won a battle in a year. We need supplies, but we also need a victory. The morale of the troops is as important to an army as weapons or supplies. Without morale, we have nothing.

GREENE: Sir, our ammunition is low.

GEORGE: By coming up on them by surprise, we'll beat them to their guns. And don't forget, we outnumber them by more than two to one.

SULLIVAN: General, I think it's a brilliant plan.

GREENE: As do I.

GEORGE: Then prepare your troops. We will mass at the river on Christmas night. In the meantime, go celebrate with your men.

★ Scene Six

NARRATOR TWO: And so George Washington, with Greene and Sullivan and twenty-four hundred men, prepared to cross the Delaware. It was a very dangerous crossing, even though the river was not very wide. The ice on the river made passing treacherous, and many boats were damaged, but none sank.

NARRATOR ONE: The crossing took much longer than George thought, but by early morning the Continental Army was across the river. Once on the New Jersey side of the Delaware River, the soldiers could hear the Hessians laughing and singing.

TOM: Listen to them, whooping it up.

FREDERICK: They've got it good.

JACK: Yes, but in the morning, they'll be too tired to fight.

GEORGE: *(walking over to the soldiers)* That is the plan, men. They'll eat too much, drink too much, and be deeply asleep by the time we're upon them. Now hush, let's not alert them to our presence.

ALL: Yes, General.

JACK: See, I told you he had a great plan!

NARRATOR TWO: By eight o'clock on the morning of December twenty-sixth, Washington's troops had the Hessian camp surrounded. With the sun barely up, George gave the order.

GEORGE: CHARGE!

FREDERICK: Wake up, you Hessians!

JACK: Attack! Attack!

TOM: Yahoo!

NARRATOR ONE: As the Continental soldiers stormed the Hessian camp, the Hessians struggled to wake up from their night of partying.

GREENE: Round them up! Round all of them up! Take the ammunition!

NARRATOR TWO: In less than one hour, the battle was over. Washington's army lost only five men, but they had captured better than nine hundred of the one thousand Hessians.

NARRATOR ONE: They were also able to take the Hessians' supplies of food, blankets, tents, and ammunition. But most important, the battle restored the sagging spirits of the Continental Army. They had scored a major victory while losing nearly nothing in return.

★ Scene Seven

NARRATOR TWO: By nightfall, George and the Continental Army had returned to their camp in Pennsylvania. Fresh from their victory, the troops celebrated.

PAUL: Three cheers for General Washington!

JACK: Hip, hip…

ALL: Hooray!

TOM: Hip, hip…

ALL: Hooray!

FREDERICK: Hip, hip—

GEORGE: *(interrupting)* Thank you, men. This was an important victory. We'll now have not only the supplies, but the strength to go on. Without this victory, we would have had to surrender. Now, at least, we have some hope.

NARRATOR ONE: They did have hope, and strength. The war would last five more years, and the Continentals would face many more tough battles with the Redcoats, not to mention another very difficult winter at Valley Forge. But the Continental Army never lost faith in George Washington. He knew their needs, and he knew how to plan battles to give the undermanned, undersupplied army the best chance.

NARRATOR TWO: And when they finally won the Battle of Yorktown, which led to the British surrender, the troops' faith in George Washington was rewarded. It was as a general that George Washington was first known as the "Father of Our Country." And it all started with his Christmas present to his troops, the Battle of Trenton.

George Washington
Teacher's Guide

Biography

George Washington was born on February 22, 1732, in Virginia. He became a surveyor at 15. In 1753 the governor of Virginia appointed him Major in the Virginia militia. He was soon promoted to Lieutenant Colonel and led a troop during the French and Indian War. By 1755 he was named commander of the entire Virginia militia.

Independently wealthy from his successful plantations, he accepted no pay for his military service to the colonies. After leading the daring Christmas day raid on the Hessian troops, Washington was able to bring his army back near his home in Virginia for the battle at Yorktown, which the British lost, ending the war.

After a brief return to Martha and Mount Vernon, Washington was soon called back to government for the Constitutional Convention of 1787. He was quickly elected to lead the convention, and when the time came to vote for president, as provided in the Constitution, one name appeared on every electoral ballot—George Washington.

As president, he established a strong central government, and put the nation on sound financial footing by establishing what became the Federal Reserve and a property tax and tariffs. While he was president, Vermont, Kentucky, and Tennessee became states. He served two terms, retired from the presidency in 1797, and died at Mount Vernon in 1799.

Classroom Activities

★ Talk About It

Before reading the play, discuss vocabulary words that may be unfamiliar, like *Hessians, Continental Army,* and *mercenary.*

Washington and his officers and his men believed that the Hessian mercenaries would not fight as well as the Redcoats themselves, who were fighting for their native land, Britain, or the Continental soldiers, who were fighting for their new land and freedom. What do your students think? Why?

Discuss the concept of a mercenary person, one who does something only for money. Does it apply to situations other than the military? Mercenary still has a negative connotation. Should it?

★ Write About It

Many of the Continental soldiers were young boys, not much older than your students. Invite students to imagine themselves as young soldiers, writing letters home to family members from a Continental Army camp along the Delaware. Students may wish to choose one of the characters in the play and write a diary entry from that person's point of view, describing the feelings and events leading up to the battle.

★ Report on It

If the Battle of Trenton had been lost, the course of the war would have been very different. The United States might not exist: America might be part of the British Commonwealth. Students might want to research British life, and report on how their lives would be different if the United States was still a part of Britain. We would use different words (*trainers* for sneakers, for example, or *pudding* for dessert), and many events in our history (the Civil War, our entry into World War I and II) would have been different or not happened at all.

George Washington • John Adams • Thomas Jefferson • James Madison • James Monroe • John Quincy Adams • Andrew Jackson • Martin Van Buren • William Henry Harrison • John Tyler • James K. Polk • Zachary Taylor • Millard Fillmore • Franklin Pierce • James Buchanan • Abraham Lincoln • Andrew Johnson • Ulysses S. Grant • Rutherford B. Hayes • James A. Garfield • Chester A. Arthur • Grover Cleveland • Benjamin Harrison • Grover Cleveland • William McKinley • Theodore Roosevelt • William H. Taft • Woodrow Wilson • Warren G. Harding • Calvin Coolidge • Herbert C. Hoover • Franklin D. Roosevelt • Harry S. Truman • Dwight D. Eisenhower • John F. Kennedy • Lyndon B. Johnson • Richard M. Nixon • Gerald R. Ford • James Earl Carter • Ronald Reagan • George Bush • William Jefferson Clinton

John Adams
The Making of a Patriot

CAST
NARRATOR ONE

NARRATOR TWO

SAMUEL ADAMS

JOHN ADAMS

ETHAN LYNCH

JUSTICE HUTCHINSON

GOVERNOR OF MASSACHUSSETS COLONY

CAPTAIN PRESTON

ABIGAIL ADAMS

★ Scene One

NARRATOR ONE: Starting in 1764, the King of England, George III, began taxing his American colonies to help pay for the cost of the French and Indian War. He passed the Stamp Act, which forced the colonists to affix a stamp to all official documents and to pay a tax on the stamp.

NARRATOR TWO: Furious at being burdened with an unfair tax, the colonists in America responded by rioting and protesting. In Massachusetts, the tax revolt was led by Samuel Adams, cousin to a young attorney named John Adams. In 1770, the king repealed the Stamp Act, but replaced it with the Townsend Acts, which taxed items the colonists needed, like glass, lead, tea, paper, and paint.

NARRATOR ONE: The king also sent his soldiers, known as Redcoats, to Boston to enforce the laws and make sure the tax was collected. The common people hated the Redcoats as much as the taxes. Again, Samuel Adams led a revolt.

(The office of John Adams in the law firm of Chief Justice Thomas Hutchinson. John Adams sits behind his desk. His cousin, Samuel Adams, stands over him.)

SAMUEL: Redcoats don't belong in Massachusetts! They take the hard-earned money out of our people's pockets and send it to a king an ocean away to pay for his wars! Our taxes should pay for things we need here! It is not fair, John, and you know it!

JOHN: I don't like the taxes any more than you do. But we won't get rid of them by running through the streets, smashing windows, destroying public order, and creating riots! Someone is going to get hurt. There are other ways to make your feelings known, Samuel.

SAMUEL: Bah! You're just worried about your reputation with your fancy friends—all supporters of the king! If you were to join up with us, it would hurt your standing with the other lawyers and judges in this colony.

NARRATOR ONE: Before John can reply, a roar is heard outside the window. The cousins run to see what's going on.

JOHN: Sam! Is this another of your riots?

SAMUEL: I swear, Cousin, I know nothing about this.

NARRATOR TWO: The cousins run down to the street, where hundreds of people are running wild. They recognize one of them.

JOHN AND SAMUEL: Ethan! What's happening?

ETHAN: The Redcoats. They're firing on the crowd! Several people were protesting the newest tax, and the Redcoats shot them dead! Come! We're going to get even.

SAMUEL: Well, Cousin, who's destroying public order now? Me? Or the Redcoats?

NARRATOR ONE: The riot that day was a result of what came to be called the Boston Massacre. A group of colonists, angry about the taxes, had thrown rocks at a group of Redcoats. The Redcoats responded by firing on the colonists, killing three and wounding seven more. Two later died of their wounds.

NARRATOR TWO: The Redcoats were arrested and charged with murder. And John Adams was assigned to defend them at their trial.

★ Scene Two

JUSTICE HUTCHINSON: John, the governor came to see me today because he wanted my best lawyer for this difficult case. That's why I brought you in.

JOHN: Thank you, sir.

GOVERNOR: I'm sure you heard about what happened between our soldiers and that mob on King Street. Well, nine of our soldiers and their commanding officer are sitting in jail. Now, as Governor, I have to try them for murder, but since I also represent the king in this colony, I am very interested in seeing that the soldiers get the best defense possible...if you understand what I mean....

JOHN: I try to give all my clients the best defense possible, sir, and I'll do the same for these men. After all, they have the right to a fair trial, and a good lawyer.

GOVERNOR: Of course, of course, Mr. Adams. Very admirable. But with the colonists in such an ugly mood, I am afraid our soldiers will not be able to get a fair trial.

JOHN: Governor, I'll try my best, but there are witnesses who saw the soldiers fire on unarmed colonists.

GOVERNOR: Unarmed! The brave soldiers merely defended themselves against a violent mob that attacked them with sticks and rocks!

JOHN: A rock is not the equal of a gun, Governor. I understand the soldiers were afraid, but that is no excuse for murder. However, I'll make sure the jury knows the crowd was throwing rocks, and hope they'll be merciful.

GOVERNOR: See that you make them understand. Good day, Mr. Adams…Mr. Hutchinson.

(The governor leaves.)

HUTCHINSON: John, I hope you understand how important this case is. Win it for the soldiers and the king will hear of it, and reward you. Lose it, and…

JOHN: I meant what I told the governor, sir. It is the right of every free man in these colonies to get a fair trial, and be represented by the best attorney he can find. That includes the Redcoats. I will see that they get their rights, but more than that I cannot do.

HUTCHINSON: I see. An honorable man. Very well. Good night, John.

★ Scene Three

(A cell in a Boston jail. John Adams visits his client, Captain Preston, to prepare the case for the defense.)

CAPTAIN PRESTON: We were on King Street, stationed there to keep public order. The tax collectors were working their way down the street. That's when the rabble started to give them trouble.

JOHN: What do you mean by "rabble"?

CAPTAIN PRESTON: You know. Rabble, the common mob—the shop owners, the sailors at the dock, the men and women who were shopping there— rabble.

JOHN: I see. By "rabble" you mean the colonists…

CAPTAIN PRESTON: *(disdainfully)* Exactly! That's what they are, after all. They get our protection, they enjoy the rights of Englishmen, then, when they have to pay their taxes, they whine and complain and riot. All the colonists are the same: lawless, whining, rabble!

JOHN: *(insulted)* I am a colonist, sir, and I am your lawyer.

CAPTAIN PRESTON: Hmph! Then you should know your lawless courts better than anyone! The rabble want to rule by riot. Well, we certainly showed them, didn't we, Mr. Lawyer?

(John gathers his papers and leaves.)

NARRATOR ONE: John began to wonder: Had it really been just self-defense? The Redcoats believed that the colonists were nothing more than lawless rabble. Was that what was really behind the shooting? John still considered himself a loyal subject of the king, so he overcame his doubts and defended the soldiers as best he could.

★ Scene Four

NARRATOR TWO: The jury, made up of wealthy landowners who were sympathetic to the king and the Redcoats, found all the soldiers innocent of murder. John Adams found favor with the governor, who invited him and his wife, Abigail, to dinner to congratulate him. The governor talked all during the meal.

GOVERNOR: I took the liberty of communicating your success to the king, John. He was most impressed.

JOHN: Thank you, sir. I was only doing my job.

GOVERNOR: We need more men like you in the colonies. And fewer like your cousin. Ha ha! *(He notices John and Abigail aren't laughing.)* Oh, come, now, Mr. and Mrs. Adams, you can't care too much for that scoundrel. How did I hear him described the other day? Oh, yes—a rabble-rouser! Ha ha!

JOHN: He is my cousin, sir, however people describe him.

GOVERNOR: Of course, of course. But his problem is that, like so many of these whining colonists, he complains about taxes and having the Redcoats here. He doesn't understand what a privilege it is to be an Englishman. Fortunately, you and I do understand what it means to be an Englishman.

JOHN: My cousin, like my wife and I, was born here in Massachusetts, sir.

GOVERNOR: Ha! An unfortunate accident of birth that you had little control over, John. I know you are one of us in your heart! And that is why the king and I want to see you in a high position. Unlike your unfortunate Cousin Rabble-rouser! The lies he tells, the way he stirs people up...Samuel Adams is a danger to us, John, but not for long. In fact, we'll soon have him in custody.

JOHN: *(confused)* What? On what charge?

GOVERNOR: Charge? The charge is whatever I say it is. That's the beauty of being governor, you see.

ABIGAIL: Wait a minute, Governor. My husband's cousin has the same rights those soldiers had—the right to a fair trial, to defend himself—

GOVERNOR: Rights, my dear, are for people who obey the law! People who pay taxes!

JOHN: Samuel and his supporters *do* pay taxes, sir. That's why they get so angry! If you and the king want this so-called disobedience to stop, then I would suggest you protect their rights. And one of those rights is the right not to be arrested without charge.

GOVERNOR: *(laughing)* Oh, I've told you, there'll be a charge. The point is to get your cousin Samuel off the streets so he can no longer make mischief or tell lies or print his news. We must show the people that his running around saying whatever he thinks will not be tolerated!

JOHN: Not tolerated? But what about freedom of speech? Freedom of assembly?

ABIGAIL: *(tugging at John's sleeve, whispering)* John, we'd better leave, before you say something you'll regret.

JOHN: Uh, your Honor, my wife is unwell. We must be going.

GOVERNOR: How unfortunate...and before we've had dessert, too. Well, all right. Good night!

★ Scene Five

(In their coach on the way home from the governor's house, John and Abigail are angry. They discuss the governor's words.)

JOHN: Abigail, it seems Samuel was right all along. The king and his powerful Redcoats are going to keep on oppressing us here in the colonies unless we fight them.

ABIGAIL: John, I'm so glad you finally see it that way. But what about Samuel? He's about to be arrested!

JOHN: Not if I can help it. *(shouting to the coach driver)* Let us off at the next corner!

ABIGAIL: That's Samuel's street.

JOHN: Right. We may just have time to warn him.

NARRATOR ONE: John and Abigail rushed to Samuel's door. He was surprised to see them, but not surprised to hear what the governor planned to do.

NARRATOR TWO: As John spoke, Samuel started to pack.

JOHN: Samuel, you were right. King George is going to abuse the colonies. He's going to tax us to death, and throw in jail anyone who disagrees with his laws. And as long as he reigns, he is not going to respect our rights. He's wrong. The soldiers who killed the townspeople were wrong. We need…we need to be free! Lead the way, Sam!

SAMUEL: Cousin, you don't know how happy I am to hear you say that. But I can't lead the fight now—I need to lie low for a while. And the colonists do need a leader. Someone respected, someone educated, someone…like you, John. Will you take my place as a leader of the revolution?

JOHN: Yes. You've convinced me.

NARRATOR ONE: John Adams became the leading voice for independence in the Massachusetts colony, and later represented Massachusetts in the Continental Congress. He persuaded Thomas Jefferson to write the Declaration of Independence, and was one of those who signed it.

NARRATOR TWO: It was this leadership in the early days of the United States that brought him from the Continental Congress to becoming George Washington's vice president, and finally to being elected the second President of the United States of America.

John Adams
Teacher's Guide

Biography

John Adams was born in Braintree, Massachussets, in 1735. He graduated from Harvard and set up a law practice in 1758. As King George passed first the Stamp Act and then the Townsend Acts, Adams, a loyal colonist, wrote articles opposing the taxes, but equally opposing violence and revolution. Until as late as 1770, he hoped there could be a peaceful resolution to the conflicts between the colonists and the crown. The Boston Massacre, however, radicalized him and he became a supporter of the revolutionary cause.

Adams was elected president in 1796. Disagreements alienated him from both political parties of the time. However, he kept the young nation out of war with France, and oversaw the transfer of power from one political party to another when he was defeated for a second term.

After retiring, he returned to Massachusetts, and died there on July 4, 1826, on the same day as Thomas Jefferson and 50 years to the day after the Declaration of Independence was passed.

Classroom Activities

★ Talk About It

Was John Adams flip-flopping on an issue when he switched sides from loyal colonist to revolutionary, or was he remaining true to a principle? Should people remain unquestioningly loyal to an idea or a side? Invite students to debate this idea. They may be able to point to personal experiences or current events to support their views.

★ Write About It

In America today, many people still object to high taxes. Sometimes their objections take extreme forms (as with separatist movements), and other times people work for tax reform through legal means. Yet most people recognize the need for some form of taxation in order to support the social organizations they approve of (like defense, education, and so forth.) Invite students to interview parents, teachers, and other adults to get their views about taxes. Interview questions should be prepared in advance and can include questions like: Are there any taxes you don't mind paying? Which programs would you be willing to do without (e.g., the space program, farm subsidies, student loans, food stamps) in order to have a tax cut? Students can analyze and present their findings in a variety of forms—graphs, posters, editorials, and so on—to share with the school community, parents, and political leaders.

★ Report on It

"Taxation without representation is tyranny!" That was the rallying cry of the Founding Fathers as they separated from Britain. What were the taxes the colonists objected to? Why? Invite students to use the library to research the meaning of this phrase, as well as the various causes of the American Revolution.

Thomas Jefferson
The Deal of the Century

CAST
NARRATOR ONE
NARRATOR TWO
THOMAS JEFFERSON
JAMES MADISON
JAMES MONROE
ROBERT LIVINGSTON
JEFFERSON'S DAUGHTERS:
    JANE, MARTHA, and LUCY

★ Scene One

(Jefferson's office. Jefferson is there with his aides Robert Livingston and James Monroe, and Secretary of State James Madison.)

NARRATOR ONE: The year is 1803. President Thomas Jefferson, a champion of small government and strict interpretation of the Constitution, is in the third year of his first term. Lately, there has been much concern over the large tract of land bordering the Mississippi River, which Spain has been forced to turn over to France.

NARRATOR TWO: At this time, the United States is a small country, extending only as far as the Mississippi. Sharing a continent with other nations has made the colonists feel uneasy, because there is no telling whether the other nations will remain friendly, or try to take over the colonies. To discuss this situation, Thomas Jefferson invites Robert Livingston, James Monroe, and his Secretary of State, James Madison, to a meeting.

JEFFERSON: Gentlemen, thank you all for coming.

MADISON: Sir, you did not mention why you asked us here. Might we know now?

JEFFERSON: James, my friend, I'm very concerned with the situation around the Mississippi River. France is in the midst of revolution. The French economy is weak. They need to raise money. My fear is that they will start charging our people who live along the river money to use it, or worse, block it off entirely.

MONROE: We, too, have been somewhat concerned. But is it really so important? After all, this is a big country.

JEFFERSON: Most of our people out on the frontier are poor farming families. That land is the only land they can afford. They get out there by carrying their belongings in a wagon. If they're lucky, they have a milking cow. And once they get out there, they usually can only build a crude cabin with a dirt roof. I think you gentlemen can imagine what happens to a dirt roof when it rains or snows.

(Madison, Livingston, and Monroe shake their heads.)

LIVINGSTON: We know the settlers don't have an easy life, but—

JEFFERSON: Once they get their cabins built, they have to chop more trees, clear the land, and start to scratch out a crop. The only way they can get that crop to market is to send it down the Mississippi River. Now, my friends, what do you think is going to happen to these good people if the French decide that the way to raise money is to charge these farmers to use the Mississippi?

LIVINGSTON: They'll have to raise prices…

MONROE: Fewer people will buy their goods…

MADISON: And there will be no trade on the western frontier.

JEFFERSON: Our economy will take a blow. The backbone of our nation is the small farmer. We all agree the federal government should have a limited role in people's lives. But part of that limited role has to be to protect people. I believe this situation falls into that category. And I believe the Constitution gives me the right to act to protect the farmers on the frontier.

MADISON, LIVINGSTON, and MONROE: Agreed!

JEFFERSON: Good. Then this is my plan. Robert, you and Monroe meet with our French friends. Tell them how important this issue is to me, and to our people. Get them to agree to allow the American settlers free use of the Mississippi and the port of New Orleans, just as they do now. And if the subject comes up, mention the possibility that, if things go well, we might be interested in purchasing New Orleans from them someday. Tell all this to Charles Talleyrand, the French minister. He is a good man, who can be trusted. Give him my regards.

MADISON: But, sir, I thought we had decided against purchasing New Orleans from the French. And anyway, the Constitution doesn't give the president the right to purchase land. In fact, Congress has "the power of the purse." And if I may say so, sir…I think you, of all people, would be most careful about overstepping your authority.

JEFFERSON: I've thought of all that. I didn't say we would definitely buy New Orleans, I just want the French to think we might. I can always say we've changed our mind later.

MONROE: I just hope they don't call your bluff, and think you're serious about buying this land you don't have the authority to buy. That could cause a lot of hard feelings and could create more problems along the frontier.

LIVINGSTON: Sir, I agree that this is risky. If the French take you up on your deal, you'll have to go before Congress to ask them to authorize money for a deal the Constitution says you don't have the power to make. I don't think it's a good—

JEFFERSON: *(interrupting)* I've known Talleyrand for a dozen years now, and I can tell you one thing—he's not going to be selling anyone any land. That's how I can make the offer—because I know he'll refuse. But the possibility of making the sale might make him agree to the other things we want! You see?

MADISON: Well, if you're sure. I just hope your plan doesn't backfire.

JEFFERSON: That would be funny, wouldn't it?

★ Scene Two

(Jefferson sits alone in his office, writing a letter.)

NARRATOR ONE: Since his wife died some years earlier, Jefferson had become very close to his grown daughters.

NARRATOR TWO: While Livingston and Monroe were off in Paris, Jefferson saw his daughters often.

(A knock at the door.)

JEFFERSON: Come in. *(The door opens and his daughters enter.)* Jane, Martha, Lucy! How good to see you. But what's wrong? Why do you look so upset?

JANE: Father, what are "implied powers"?

JEFFERSON: Where did you hear that expression?

MARTHA: In one of the newspapers in Boston, they were saying that you didn't have the courage to use your "implied powers" to help the country.

LUCY: Of course, we marched right over there and demanded an explanation. Being newspapermen, they naturally did not give us a very polite answer!

JANE: So, Father, will you give us an answer? What are implied powers?

JEFFERSON: Implied powers are powers that some people think the president has, even though the Constitution doesn't mention them. Some people feel that if the Constitution doesn't say you can't do something, then it "implies" that you can do it. But I think we should follow the Constitution just as it is written. I believe the only way we can protect the rights of all the people, and prevent presidents from doing whatever they want, like kings, is to stick to the words of the Constitution. In all my political career, I have never supported the idea of using these so-called "implied" powers.

MARTHA: So that's what the newspaper was complaining about. They want you to do something that the Constitution doesn't specifically say you can do.

JEFFERSON: That's correct.

(There is a knock at the door. Livingston and Monroe enter.)

JEFFERSON: Robert! James! Back from Paris so soon? Why didn't you write to say you would be returning?

LIVINGSTON: Mr. President, we must speak with you immediately. Hello, ladies.

MARTHA: We were just leaving, gentlemen. See you tonight, Father. *(The daughters exit.)*

JEFFERSON: See you then, girls.

MONROE: Well, we met with Talleyrand. The economy in France is very bad now, sir. Much worse than we thought.

LIVINGSTON. The French government needs to raise cash—right away!

JEFFERSON: Uh-oh. They called our bluff. They want to sell us New Orleans.

MONROE: Well, not exactly. They do want to sell us land. All of it.

LIVINGSTON: Talleyrand wants to sell us the Louisiana Territory.

JEFFERSON: That would double the size of the United States.

MONROE: Yes. And it would ensure the safety and economy of the settlers.

LIVINGSTON: And he's only asking four cents an acre.

JEFFERSON: *(quickly multiplying in his head)* That comes to about fifteen million dollars! It sounds like a lot. But it would really be a bargain.

MONROE: That's what we thought, sir. Let's agree to buy it right away, before Talleyrand raises his price.

JEFFERSON: I...I don't know. It would protect the farmers, no doubt, but I cannot abandon what we believe the government should be just because it's a good deal.

MONROE: But this is an incredible deal.

LIVINGSTON: Mr. President, I have learned as a diplomat that the best deals are the deals that have something in it for everyone. We get our land, we can patrol it with our own army and regulate it with our own laws, while the French make money. It fits the definition of a good deal.

JEFFERSON: But there is nothing in the Constitution that gives the President the power to buy land, no matter how good the reasons.

MONROE: But there is nothing that says he can't either.

LIVINGSTON: It is truly up to you, Thomas.

JEFFERSON: When does Talleyrand need an answer?

LIVINGSTON: Today is Friday. We return to Paris on Monday.

JEFFERSON: Then I will give you an answer by then.

★ Scene Three

NARRATOR ONE: That evening Jefferson dined with his daughters. He hardly spoke while he ate.

MARTHA: Father, what's wrong? You haven't said a word all through dinner.

JEFFERSON: This offer to buy the Louisiana Territory troubles me. If I turn the French down, then they are just going to make the deal with another nation, and that is going to put our people in danger. But if I do make the purchase, I risk looking like a hypocrite.

LUCY: Why?

JEFFERSON: When we wrote the Constitution, I always argued that the federal government should not do too much. A government by the people should be run by the people, and the President shouldn't impose his wishes on them.

JANE: But didn't the people elect you President?

JEFFERSON: Yes.

MARTHA: And they get another chance to vote for you next election, don't they?

JEFFERSON: Of course.

MARY: So if they don't like the job you're doing, they can make someone else the president.

LUCY: So if the people have the ultimate power to remove you, and you accept their decision, then you don't have the power over them, do you?

JEFFERSON: I guess not. But what is the basis for making a land deal?

LUCY: Defending the farmers. And besides, it is for the good of the nation.

MARY: It's still the same government by the people.

JEFFERSON: So I should make this deal.

MARTHA: Father, you're getting four cents an acre. What are we talking about?

JEFFERSON: I guess you're right. Well, girls, we just doubled the size of the country. A toast.

(They raise their glasses.)

MARTHA: Now this is more like a dinner with Father.

★ Scene Four

NARRATOR TWO: They next day, Jefferson announced his decision.

JEFFERSON: Robert, James, go to Paris and tell Talleyrand to make the deal.

MADISON: Sir, may I speak? I don't see where the Constitution gives you the right to buy land. And we are committed to a strict reading of the Constitution.

JEFFERSON: James, we wrote that document to last. We can't expect it to cover every possibility that will come up over the years and years the future holds. We can only do what we think is the best for the country. Let's get the land and let our people govern it. If the people think I've changed my principles, then they will give someone else the job. That's the difference between us and royalty. If the people don't like the king, they have nowhere to go. If they don't like us, they can go the ballot box. That's what makes us different. That's what makes us a democracy.

MADISON: I see your point.

JEFFERSON: Mr. Livingston, Mr. Monroe, we'll take the land for four cents an acre, and with our best regards to the good people of France. Now go.

LIVINGSTON: Yes, sir!

MONROE: Yes, sir!

NARRATOR: The deal for the Louisiana Purchase was completed in 1803, and Jefferson was re-elected in 1804. The people who elected Jefferson agreed that he had acted for the good of the country. And today we agree. The Louisiana Purchase started a wave of growth in America that the Founding Fathers could never have predicted. It set the stage for America to grow into the great nation it is today. And the credit can go to the great thinking of a great man: Thomas Jefferson, who always put the people first.

Thomas Jefferson
Teacher's Guide

Biography

Thomas Jefferson was born in Virginia in 1742. He considered himself a philosopher and inventor, rather than a politician or leader. Despite this, he became a member of the Virginia House of Burgesses in 1769, and a member of the Continental Congress in 1774. At 33, he was the youngest member of the congress, but as the best writer, it was he who was selected to write the Declaration of Independence.

President George Washington named Jefferson the country's first secretary of state. Jefferson was elected president in 1800, and reelected by a landslide in 1804. Jefferson oversaw the transition of power from one political party to another, approved the Louisiana Purchase, which doubled the size of the country and solved foreign policy crises involving the Barbary Pirates.

Retiring from the presidency in 1808, he was succeeded by James Madison. Among Jefferson's many accomplishments were the design of his home, Monticello, the establishment of the University of Virginia, and inventions that included the pantograph and a revolving table. Thomas Jefferson died on the Fourth of July in 1826, the exact same day that John Adams died.

Classroom Activities

★ Talk About It

Familiarize students with the U.S. Constitution. Discuss what is meant by "implied powers" and the different ways to interpret the Constitution mentioned in the play. Jefferson favored a strict interpretation, others a looser one. What is the difference? Which would students favor? Role-play with students, taking and supporting different positions. Do they think that in today's world a strict interpretation of the Constitution would benefit our society or hinder progress?

★ Write About It

Currently, many Americans have a renewed interest in constitutional issues, with many people taking the position that the federal government has become "too big," and that individual states' and citizens' rights are being overridden. Invite students to use their prior knowledge and the research they've done in connection with this play in order to clarify and write about their feelings on this issue.

They may want to take a single issue, like gun control, and write an essay or speech that states their position and the constitutional support for legislation about it. This activity should show that our Constitution can be interpreted in many different ways, and give students an appreciation for the difficulties our elected officials have when making laws that must fit with the Constitution.

★ Report on It

The debate over the Louisiana Purchase raised the question of what the powers of the president are. Have students research what the Constitution says about the executive, legislative, and judicial branches, and the checks and balances the Founding Fathers provided for each. Have them draw their own conclusions about the Louisiana Purchase: Did Jefferson act within the Constitution or overstep his authority? Invite students to debate their findings.

Alternatively, once students are familiar with the Constitution, invite them to look through newspapers or watch national news broadcasts to become aware of constitutional issues that are currently being debated. Students can keep a clipping file of "Constitutional Currents" to provide research material for debate and writing on constitutional issues.

George Washington • John Adams • Thomas Jefferson • James Madison • James Monroe • John Quincy Adams • Andrew Jackson • Martin Van Buren • William Henry Harrison • John Tyler • James K. Polk • Zachary Taylor • Millard Fillmore • Franklin Pierce • James Buchanan • Abraham Lincoln • Andrew Johnson • Ulysses S. Grant • Rutherford B. Hayes • James A. Garfield • Chester A. Arthur • Grover Cleveland • Benjamin Harrison • Grover Cleveland • William McKinley • Theodore Roosevelt • William H. Taft • Woodrow Wilson • Warren G. Harding • Calvin Coolidge • Herbert C. Hoover • Franklin D. Roosevelt • Harry S. Truman • Dwight D. Eisenhower • John F. Kennedy • Lyndon B. Johnson • Richard M. Nixon • Gerald R. Ford • James Earl Carter • Ronald Reagan • George Bush • William Jefferson Clinton

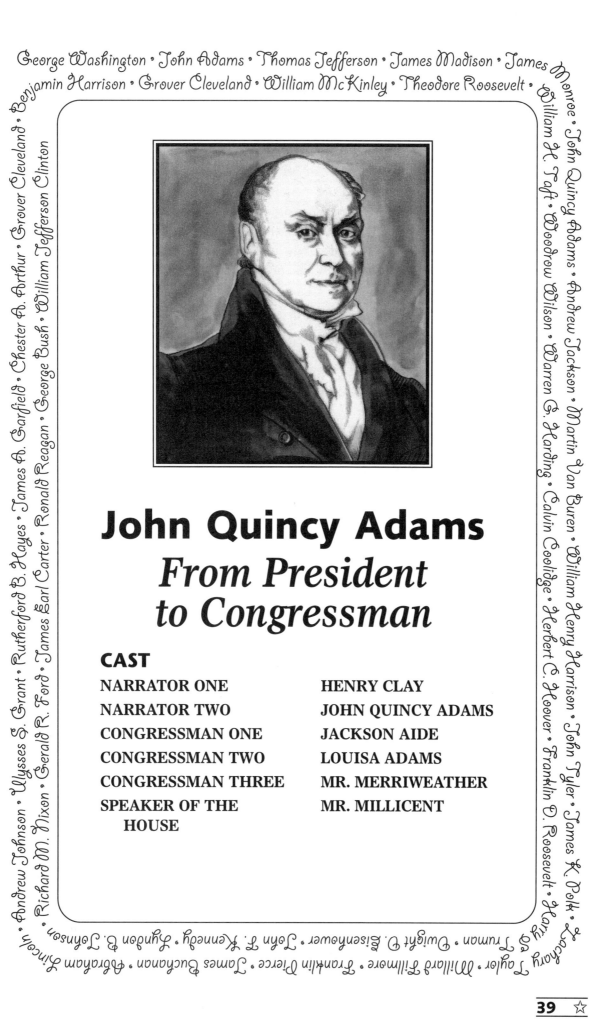

John Quincy Adams
From President to Congressman

CAST

NARRATOR ONE

NARRATOR TWO

CONGRESSMAN ONE

CONGRESSMAN TWO

CONGRESSMAN THREE

SPEAKER OF THE
  HOUSE

HENRY CLAY

JOHN QUINCY ADAMS

JACKSON AIDE

LOUISA ADAMS

MR. MERRIWEATHER

MR. MILLICENT

★ Scene One

NARRATOR ONE: In 1824 four men ran for president under the Democratic-Republican ticket—John Quincy Adams, who was then secretary of state under President James Monroe; Henry Clay, a senator; General Andrew Jackson; and William Crawford of Georgia, who suffered a stroke early in the campaign. When the votes were all finally counted, no candidate had achieved the necessary number of electoral votes. According to the Constitution, when this happens, the election goes to the House of Representatives, which then elects the president.

CONGRESSMAN ONE: Jackson's my man!

CONGRESSMAN TWO: Making Jackson the president will be the death of this country! He's a madman! I'm voting for Adams.

CONGRESSMAN ONE: Jackson is a man of the people! Adams is a snob and so are you!

CONGRESSMAN THREE: Gentlemen, please! Henry Clay is the man for the job. He's not a snob like Mr. Adams, and he's not a madman like General Jackson. I would advise you to cast your votes for our colleague from the Senate.

SPEAKER OF THE HOUSE: The House will come to order. Gentlemen, please take your seats. We will now undertake this very serious matter of electing a president. The sergeant at arms will take the first ballot.

NARRATOR TWO: The first vote was taken and although Jackson held a slight lead, it wasn't enough to make a majority. Another vote was taken, with the same result. Then Henry Clay took to the Senate floor.

CLAY: My dear colleagues in the House, after much contemplation I have decided to withdraw from the race for the presidency, and further, I ask all of you who voted for me to instead cast your votes for Secretary of State John Quincy Adams!

CONGRESSMAN THREE: Henry, what are you doing?

CLAY: I don't want Andrew Jackson to become the president. This is the only way.

NARRATOR ONE: With Clay's votes boosting him, Adams was elected on the next ballot. Adams then made Clay his secretary of state. Though Clay maintained he did what he did to keep Jackson from the White House, many, including Jackson's supporters, charged Clay and Adams with making a deal. Jackson continued making the charge throughout Adams' presidency.

NARRATOR TWO: In 1828 Jackson again ran for president. He called the Adams-Clay deal a "corrupt bargain" and the people believed him. John Quincy Adams lost the election of 1828.

★ Scene Two

NARRATOR ONE: On his last day as president, John Quincy Adams packed up his office with Henry Clay and Louisa, his wife.

JOHN: My last day as President. It's a strange feeling.

CLAY: Last day for now. You can run again in four years, and this time you'll beat that lunatic.

JOHN: General Jackson is not a lunatic. Just a little rough around the edges.

CLAY: He's rabble from the get-go.

JOHN: I remember the English in Boston telling my father the same thing about us once. *(He tosses a book in a box.)* I'm glad Father wasn't alive to see this day.

CLAY: Don't fool yourself, John. Your father would be proud of you. You'll be looking like the savior of the nation after they have Jackson as president for four years. He's quite mad, you know. He wiped out all those Indians in Florida. He even had his own men killed for the smallest offenses!

JOHN: Unsubstantiated rumor. The fight is over, Henry. Enough of the bitterness.

CLAY: John, your life is here. Right here. Washington, D.C. Government. It's your family tradition.

JOHN: My family tradition seems to be losing. Well, it looks like we're heading home, Henry. Try to keep Mr. Jackson from giving the store away.

(There is a knock on the door.)

JOHN: Enter.

(An aide for Andrew Jackson enters.)

JOHN: Yes?

AIDE: General Jackson has had his things outside for many hours and he would like to know when he can move in.

JOHN: Tell the General I'm leaving as fast as I can.

AIDE: He is in a hurry, Mr. Adams.

CLAY: He's still Mr. President today, young man.

AIDE: Oh yes, of course.

(The aide leaves.)

CLAY: Just like the General to have an obnoxious young man like *that* working for him.

JOHN: Louisa, I think it's time we took our leave of this city.

LOUISA: I think you're right, and with good riddance.

★ Scene Three

NARRATOR ONE: John Quincy Adams returned home to Boston a disappointed man. It took quite a while for him to recover from his loss.

(Adams's home in Massachusetts. John and Louisa are sitting in front of a fireplace, reading. It is early 1830.)

JOHN: *(closing his book)* Louisa, I'm bored. I just don't seem to find anything fulfilling these days. I miss government.

LOUISA: That's only natural. After all, your father was president, you were president, and your family practically invented this government.

JOHN: It's strange, because I didn't think very much of government when I was down in Washington. The deals, the behind-the-scenes maneuvers, the bitter fights, the lies people told about us, and the lies we told about other people. It all made me feel so…tired and dispirited.

LOUISA: It wasn't as bad as all that. And now you feel bored… I think you need to come out of retirement and run for office again. Run for senate or for governor.

JOHN: That would be like a landowner selling his land to work the fields like a laborer. It wouldn't make sense!

LOUISA: Well, write a book about your experiences.

JOHN: I have no desire to write a book, and even if I did, who would buy it? Judging by the election results, nobody cares about John Quincy Adams. It's Andrew Jackson the people want.

LOUISA: I'm not so sure about that. The other day, when my friends were here, all they could talk about was how beastly that man is. Do you know Mrs. Millicent, from Brookline? She and her husband attended the inauguration, and she said General Jackson invited practically everybody who voted for him. So there they were in Washington—a drunken, unruly mob, following President Jackson right into the White House! They broke plates, tore curtains, smashed windows, and drank all the liquor in sight. It was very difficult to get them to leave the White House afterward! That's the sort of person running our government these days.

JOHN: Well, that's who the American people voted for. That's what they want. We have to accept that.

LOUISA: I accept that, but I don't share your view that Andrew Jackson is more popular than you. He's not popular here in New England, that's for sure!

(There is a knock on the door. Louisa opens it. Mr. Merriweather and Mr. Millicent, two merchants from Boston, enter.)

MERRIWEATHER and MILLICENT: Good evening, Mrs. Adams, John.

LOUISA: Good evening. Won't you come in?

JOHN: What brings you gentlemen here?

MILLICENT: Well, John, I'm sure you are aware the disarray our current president has thrown the government into.

JOHN: I heard a few stories.

MERRIWEATHER: John, it's terrible. He has closed the Bank of the United States, he's chased the Indians out of Florida, he won't meet with his Cabinet, and he vetoes everything that comes to his desk! It's just awful.

JOHN: He seems very popular with the people, though.

MILLICENT: Oh, maybe out in the bushes, where he comes from.

JOHN: *(sternly)* Remember, those are still American bushes.

MERRIWEATHER: But here in New England—

MILLICENT: John, the president's policies are going to spell ruin for this region. Without the Bank of the United States to regulate commerce and help enforce the rules, we're going to have chaos.

MERRIWEATHER: No one will sell us materials, because our money will be worthless. Without materials we can't manufacture anything. We'll be ruined! And that's not all—

JOHN: Gentlemen, I agree that Jackson will be bad for our region, and bad for the country, but I don't see what I can do about it. After all, the American people—even those out in what you call "the bushes"—have chosen Mr. Jackson. They don't want me. They want him and his policies. So I hope you're not here to ask me to run for president, because I won't do it.

MERRIWEATHER: Good, because that's not what we're here to ask you.

MILLICENT: The congressional seat from this district is about to open up. We need a good man to represent this area in Congress.

JOHN: And you would like me to recommend someone?

MERRIWEATHER: Oh, no, we already have someone in mind!

MILLICENT: You!

JOHN: Me? I am a former President of the United States! For me to now run for Congress…wouldn't that be a bit odd!?

LOUISA: John, I think it would be wonderful! I know it would be a little strange to have a former president in Congress. I know it might feel like what you said before, like a landowner going to work as a laborer. Yet think of the experience you could bring to the job. Think of the influence you could have in the House of Representatives!

JOHN: But there are so many members of Congress. I'd be just a face in the crowd.

MERRIWEATHER: But that's the point—as a former president, you wouldn't be. You'd be a leader.

JOHN: I must think about this. But I thank you for your generous offer. Now if you will excuse me…

MERRIWEATHER and MILLICENT: *(together)* Of course. Good night, sir.

(They leave.)

JOHN: Louisa, what would my father say to such an idea?

LOUISA: If I knew your father at all, I think he would have been flattered by how highly his neighbors thought of him. And I think he would have been compelled to serve. That is what Adamses seem to do best, after all.

JOHN: He was in the same position, cast out of the White House after only one term.

LOUISA: Yes, and he sat in his house, bored and unhappy, and waited for someone to give him something to do. Yet because everyone thought of him as "the Great Former President, John Adams," they were afraid to approach him. So he died, waiting to be needed. Waiting for a call that never came. You are lucky, John. You've just received that call. Your neighbors and fellow citizens need you.

JOHN: You don't think I'd seem ridiculous, going back to Washington as a mere congressman after having been president?

LOUISA: I think you would seem like a man whose neighbors respect him. I think you'd seem like a great American.

JOHN: You know, Louisa, if I run—I might not win.

LOUISA: You'll never know unless you try. But I have faith in our neighbors. I believe you'll win.

JOHN: All right, I'll run. But if I win, and we have to move back to Washington, I don't want to hear any complaints about how hot Washington is in the summer!

(They both laugh.)

LOUISA: I promise, *no* complaints.

NARRATOR ONE: John Quincy Adams did run for Congress. He was elected to the House of Representatives in 1831, and served there until 1848. While there, he helped draft many bills that dealt with the national bank and other issues he had worked for while president.

NARRATOR TWO: In 1844 he successfully led the fight to repeal the "gag" rule, which kept slavery issues from being discussed. In 1848, he suffered a stroke on the floor of the House, while debating a bill. He died two days later. His colleagues said he died in the place he loved most— the government of the United States.

John Quincy Adams
Teacher's Guide

Biography

John Quincy Adams, son of the second president, John Adams, was born on July 11, 1767, in Braintree (later renamed Quincy, in his honor), Massachussets. Early in his career, Adams served as a U.S. diplomat ministering to Russia, France, and England.

While serving President James Monroe as secretary of state, Adams developed the foreign policy that was to become known as the Monroe Doctrine, which warned Europe against further colonization of North America.

Adams did not believe in political patronage, and so, as president, he did not stock his cabinet with his supporters. Many, in turn, attacked him, and supported his rival, Andrew Jackson, which undermined Adams's power as president.

Adams lost the presidential election of 1828, but returned to Washington as a congressman in 1830. He suffered a stroke while on the floor of the House in 1848, and died two days later.

Classroom Activities

★ Talk About It

John Quincy Adams's supporters in Boston were afraid of President Andrew Jackson, a southerner. They were horrified by what they considered his and his supporters' uncouth ways, and fearful he would not represent their interests. There are parallels today. Some Americans distrust those who live in another region, or who have a background or follow an ideology that is diferent from theirs.

Students may be interested to discuss the wide spectrum of ideologies and local interests that Americans around the country support. (Examples might include urban versus rural interests, needs of the young versus those of the aged, advocates of gun control versus those who support gun ownership, etc.). You might want to discuss with students the idea that a president must serve the interests of the whole country, not just those of his own region, or of the people who elected him. Discuss also the idea that America is a "big tent," with lots of different people with varying points of view—but all of whom are, first and foremost, Americans.

★ Report on It

In the play, John Quincy Adams's supporters characterize Andrew Jackson and his followers in extremely negative ways. The parties regularly do that to each other today. Statements made by politicians and political ads, especially during an election year, are often examples of this "mudslinging." As the play points out, and research bears out, it's not a modern phenomenon.

Invite interested students to research old newspapers and nonfiction books to learn about negative campaigning from the earliest days of our nation's history. Questions to think about while researching include: Why is it done? Does one party resort to it more than another? Is it on the increase? Who is to blame?

★ Write About It

Encourage students to present their research findings to class in a variety of formats, including oral reports, essays, charts, posters, graphs of the use of negative ads, and surveys of voters (parents, teachers, and other adults) to find out what they think of negative ads, why they believe they're used, what they suppose their effects are, etc.

Students might write to elected officials asking them to reject negative advertising, or they might create their own positive ads for a school election or mock election.

George Washington • John Adams • Thomas Jefferson • James Madison • James Monroe • John Quincy Adams • Andrew Jackson • Martin Van Buren • William Henry Harrison • John Tyler • James K. Polk • Zachary Taylor • Millard Fillmore • Franklin Pierce • James Buchanan • Abraham Lincoln • Andrew Johnson • Ulysses S. Grant • Rutherford B. Hayes • James A. Garfield • Chester A. Arthur • Grover Cleveland • Benjamin Harrison • Grover Cleveland • William McKinley • Theodore Roosevelt • William H. Taft • Woodrow Wilson • Warren G. Harding • Calvin Coolidge • Herbert C. Hoover • Franklin D. Roosevelt • Harry S. Truman • Dwight D. Eisenhower • John F. Kennedy • Lyndon B. Johnson • Richard M. Nixon • Gerald R. Ford • James Earl Carter • Ronald Reagan • George Bush • William Jefferson Clinton

Abraham Lincoln
Keeping the Country United

CAST
NARRATOR ONE
NARRATOR TWO
LIBRARIAN
TOMMY CUNNINGHAM
ABRAHAM LINCOLN
GENERAL GEORGE MEADE
MARY LINCOLN
MRS. EARLE

★ Scene One

NARRATOR ONE: Tommy Cunningham is sitting in his school library trying to work on his school report. The topic he chose is the Gettysburg Address.

NARRATOR TWO: And the report is due tomorrow.

LIBRARIAN: How's it going, Tommy?

TOMMY: Terrible! I'm sorry I picked this topic—The Gettysburg Address. Say, you're not the regular librarian. How did you know my name?

LIBRARIAN: I'm the assistant librarian. And I know a lot of things that would surprise you.

TOMMY: Do you know anything about Abraham Lincoln and the Gettysburg Address?

LIBRARIAN: I might. What do you need to know about it?

TOMMY: Everything: like why he made it, and what it means, and—

LIBRARIAN: Oh, that's easy. And interesting.

TOMMY: These books sure don't make it sound interesting. I can hardly understand all this "Four score and seven years ago" stuff! And why do they call it the "Gettysburg Address"? It sounds like the number of a house.

LIBRARIAN: *(gently laughing)* Ha ha! Well, Tommy, an address isn't just a house number. When you address people, it means you speak right to them, like the president did when he gave that speech. And, well, maybe it would be easier to show you why he made it, instead of telling you.

TOMMY: Show me? How?

LIBRARIAN: You'll see. Follow me.

★ Scene Two

NARRATOR ONE: Tommy follows the librarian into Mrs. Earle's office. Suddenly everything looks very different from what he expected.

NARRATOR TWO: Tommy and the librarian stand atop a ridge overlooking a field. There is devastation everywhere.

NARRATOR ONE: The trees and grass are burned. Parts of cannons that had been blasted to bits are strewn around. Shirts and boots that had been worn by Union and Confederate soldiers are on the ground. The acrid smell of smoke fills the air. Tommy becomes scared.

LIBRARIAN: You all right, Tommy?

TOMMY: Yeah. This is a scary place.

LIBRARIAN: Battlefields, even when the battle is over, are haunting. Do you know what day this is?

TOMMY: No.

LIBRARIAN: It's the Fourth of July, 1863. But nobody feels like celebrating. The battle of Gettysburg ended yesterday.

TOMMY: Wow.

LIBRARIAN: This hill we're standing on is called Cemetery Ridge. The Confederate soldiers charged right into the middle of the Union line. Seven thousand men died.

TOMMY: Seven thousand men. How horrible!

LIBRARIAN: Yes, it was a horrible loss of life. But many of these soldiers died for a reason: to keep the country together. They died so the nation could survive.

TOMMY: Gosh. *(looks around)* Can we leave now?

LIBRARIAN: Yes, we can. I don't like it here much either.

★ Scene Three

NARRATOR TWO: Tommy and the librarian go back through the door. But instead of the school library, they find themselves inside President Lincoln's office. He is there with the Union commander, General George Meade.

NARRATOR ONE: General Meade has turned back General Lee's army at Gettysburg.

LINCOLN: The people of the United States owe you a great debt, General Meade.

MEADE: Thank you, Mr. President. But the soldiers who died made the greatest sacrifice.

LINCOLN: Yes, they did. And when the army dedicates that cemetery on the Gettysburg battlefield, I intend to be there to pay my respects.

MEADE: Mr. President, may I speak freely?

LINCOLN: You may.

MEADE: Mr. President, I don't know if that's a good idea. The people attending that dedication will be the relatives of the men who died in the battle. They don't understand why their sons, brothers, and husbands had to die. And they blame you. Some of them don't want anything more to do with you, or with this war. They're ready to give up!

LINCOLN: General Meade, the United States is the most unique nation on earth. It is the only one where all men are created equal, where it doesn't matter how rich or important your family is. And where it doesn't matter what race your family is. We are all equal. And we're the only nation on this planet that believes that, and built it's government on that belief. Without this war, we wouldn't be that nation anymore. Those men died so that this nation, this great nation, could live. I don't know how the war is going to end, I don't know what is going to happen to the nation after the war, but I do know why your men died. And as the President, I have to make sure everyone knows. There can be no doubt.

MEADE: *(impressed)* Mr. President, if anyone can make the people understand, you can.

LINCOLN: Thank you. *(He sits down, deep in thought.)*

NARRATOR: Meade left the room. After a minute, Mary Todd, Lincoln's wife, entered.

MARY: Abraham?

LINCOLN: Mary, my dear, come in.

MARY: You seem so sad.

LINCOLN: Mary, you're the only one I can tell my true feelings to… I tried to seem confident in front of General Meade, but I'm worried.

MARY: Worried about what?

LINCOLN: Everyone wants to know what's going to happen to the country. They look to the president when they feel uncertain. I remember when I was fighting in the Black Hawk War, I always looked in the newspaper to see what the president was saying. He was my leader.

MARY: I did the same thing.

LINCOLN: Except now I'm the president. The soldiers and the people are looking at me that same way. And I don't know if I can do it.

MARY: Do you know what the people are looking for? They're looking for someone to follow, who will lead them through the trouble to a place that's safe. That's what they want you to do.

LINCOLN: But can I do that?

MARY: Yes, you can. If you keep them together, they will follow you. And you can then lead them to the right place.

LINCOLN: But what if I lead them to the wrong place?

MARY: You won't. Because you're a good man. And because what the country is all about means too much to you. If they follow you, it is because you do know where to take the country. That is why they voted for you. That is why they want you as their leader.

LINCOLN: They don't seem to want me right now.

MARY: They're troubled. People always are when they don't know what's going to happen. They get worried, they get angry. That's when they need a strong leader. That's when they need someone to give them the will to go on.

LINCOLN: But what if I don't have the will to go on?

TOMMY: Abe! Abe! Don't worry! You're one of our greatest presidents.

LIBRARIAN: He can't hear you.

TOMMY: But why is he so worried? Doesn't he know he's our greatest president!?

LIBRARIAN: *(smiling)* You know that because you're standing here, one hundred years later. But Mr. Lincoln knows that if the Union loses, if he can't inspire the people to go on fighting for unity, well, Abraham Lincoln could be the last President of the United States.

TOMMY: Gosh. *(Turning back to the scene in Lincoln's office.)*

MARY: Go to Gettysburg. Make your speech. Remind the people why their loved ones died, and why we still need to go on fighting. You'll restore their faith. And you'll keep the country together.

LINCOLN: Yes. I'll go. I just hope they'll listen.

NARRATOR ONE: Tommy and the librarian turn to go. But when they walk out of Lincoln's office, another strange scene unfolds before them.

★ Scene Four

NARRATOR TWO: Tommy and the librarian are on the same ridge they were standing on before. This time, it is a little less devastated. But where there had been trees and grass, there are now gravestones, thousands of them, as far as the eye could see.

NARRATOR ONE: There is also a large crowd of people standing around the gravestones. Tommy and the librarian are at the back of the crowd. They can see a stage draped with American flags at the front. Tommy sees President Lincoln on the stage. The date is November 19, 1863.

NARRATOR TWO: As Lincoln walks to the front of the stage, most of the crowd is quiet.

TOMMY: Why aren't they applauding? He's the president!

LIBRARIAN: Remember, he's not very popular with these people right now. These are the ones whose relatives died in the battle.

TOMMY: Oh… right.

NARRATOR ONE: Lincoln is nervous as he starts to speak to the angry crowd.

LINCOLN: Thank you, ladies and gentlemen, fellow Americans, honored guests. Fourscore and seven years ago our fathers brought forth on this continent a new nation …conceived in liberty and dedicated to the proposition that all men are created equal.

TOMMY: Hey! This is it! This is the Gettysburg Address! And that's what he said to General Meade—

LIBRARIAN: Sshh! Listen…

LINCOLN: Now we are engaged in a great civil war, testing whether that nation or any nation so conceived and so dedicated can long endure.

TOMMY: Ohhh! I get it. He's telling them he's worried the country won't last.

LIBRARIAN: Yes, now hush!

LINCOLN: We are met on a great battlefield of that war. We have come to dedicate a portion of that field as a final resting place for those who here gave their lives that the nation might live. It is altogether fitting and proper that we should do this. But in a larger sense, we cannot dedicate, we cannot consecrate, we cannot hallow this ground. The brave men, living and dead, who struggled here have consecrated it far above our poor power to add or detract.

TOMMY: *(interrupting)* I get it now. He's saying we can't dedicate the cemetery 'cause it's already been dedicated—by the soldiers who gave their lives for their cause!

LIBRARIAN *(whispering):* Right!

LINCOLN: The world will little note nor long remember what we say here, but it can never forget what they did here. It is for us the living rather to be dedicated here to the unfinished work which they who fought here have thus far so nobly advanced. It is rather for us to be here dedicated to the great task remaining before us—that from these honored dead we take increased devotion to that cause for which they gave the last full measure of devotion—that we here highly resolve that these dead shall not have died in vain, that this nation under God shall have a new birth of freedom, and that government of the people, by the people, for the people shall not perish from the earth.

NARRATOR TWO: Up on stage, Lincoln sits down. The crowd, which had expected a long, boring speech, is silent for a second. Then, moved by the president's speech, they start to applaud.

NARRATOR ONE: Cheering begins. It continues loud and long. The crowd applauds the president many times.

NARRATOR TWO: Through the cheering, Tommy hears a bell ringing, and a voice calling his name.

 ★ Scene Five

MRS. EARLE: Tommy…Tommy, wake up. The bell's rung. Time for class.

TOMMY: Huh? What?

MRS. EARLE: You fell asleep.

TOMMY: Mrs. Earle …I…I thought you were out today.

MRS. EARLE: *(laughs)* No, I'm standing right here.

TOMMY: No, you're out for the day, and your substitute took me to the White House and Cemetery Ridge, and then we heard Abraham Lincoln give the Gettysburg Address …and I understood it all!

MRS. EARLE: Tommy, you must have been dreaming. Now you better get to class before you're late.

TOMMY: Yes, Mrs. Earle.

NARRATOR ONE: Tommy gathers his books and belongings. He hears Mrs. Earle tallking to her new assistant.

MRS. EARLE: Now remember, fiction is on the right, history on the left. Do you understand, Mr.…?

LIBRARIAN: *(quickly)* Oh, you can just call me Abe.

MRS. EARLE: Fine.

NARRATOR TWO: Tommy thinks he's hearing things, until he looks back and sees the assistant librarian putting books away.

TOMMY: Excuse me, is your name Abe?

LIBRARIAN: Yes, it is.

TOMMY: *(puzzled)* And this is your first day here?

LIBRARIAN: *(smiling)* Yes.

TOMMY: *(shakes his head and starts to walk away)* Oh, okay. I guess it was a dream.

LIBRARIAN: Tommy? *(Tommy freezes.)*

TOMMY: Y…Y..yes?

LIBRARIAN: Do you understand what the Gettysburg Address is all about now?

TOMMY: *(wide-eyed)* Yes, yes sir, Mr. Lincoln.

Abraham Lincoln
Teacher's Guide

Biography

Abraham Lincoln was born in Kentucky on February 12, 1809. His mother died when he was nine years old, and his father, Thomas, remarried in 1819. Lincoln grew very fond of his stepmother, Sarah Johnson, who taught him to read and write.

Lincoln became a lawyer in 1836. As early as 1837, he stated his opposition to slavery. He married Mary Todd in 1842, and in 1847 served one term in the U.S. House of Representatives. By 1858 his opposition to the expansion of slavery prompted him to run for the United States Senate against popular Democrat Stephen Douglas.

The Republicans nominated Lincoln for president in 1860. Fearing the antislavery policies of the Republicans, seven southern states promised to secede if Lincoln were elected. One month after Lincoln was sworn in, the Confederate forces fired on Fort Sumter, South Carolina, and the Civil War had begun. Lacking military experience, Lincoln relied on his generals for military direction. However, the strong leaders were all on the side of the South, including the best general in America, Robert E. Lee. The Union army lacked direction until it defeated the Confederates at Gettysburg, and General Ulysses Grant scored a Union victory at Vicksburg.

Lincoln then appointed Grant as army commander, and the Union won the war in 1865. Lincoln was shot by John Wilkes Booth on April 15, 1865, five days after Lee surrendered, and died the next day.

Classroom Activities

★ Talk About It

Invite students to discuss the language of the Gettysburg Address, which is very different from language used today. Some vocabulary and sentence structure may be difficult for students to understand without assistance, as may some expressions like the opening line, "Fourscore and seven years ago." They may have questions like: "How many years is a 'score'?" or "What 'fathers' is Lincoln referring to?"

Once students understand the speech, ask: What do they think of his message? Do they agree or disagree?

★ Write About It

After students have discussed the address and understand what it means, invite them to rewrite it in today's language.

★ Report on It

Invite interested students to rehearse and read aloud their Gettysburg Address to other classes. As an extension, invite them to research, write, and deliver speeches on the slavery issue from various points of view. For example, one student might adopt the persona of an emancipated slave, another, that of a southern plantation owner; a slave; a northern abolitionist; and so on.

You may also want to have students investigate other important speeches, such as Martin Luther King, Jr.'s "I Have a Dream" speech, Sojourner Truth's "Ain't I a Woman?" speech, FDR's "Nothing to Fear but Fear Itself" speech, John F. Kennedy's inaugural address, or Ronald Reagan's "Morning in America" speech. Discuss how speeches have changed in modern political and social life, and invite speculation as to the reasons why there are so few modern speeches or speakers of note. Has anything taken the place of the speech as the vehicle for transmitting a leader's ideas?

Theodore Roosevelt
City Slicker Goes West

CAST

SKIP WAKEFIELD (THE NARRATOR)

**MEMBERS OF THE NORTH DAKOTA MAPPING
   CREW (TOM, GEORGE, PHIL, PETEY)**

JOE BAYLESS

YOUNG SKIP

THEODORE ROOSEVELT (TR)

EDITH CAROW

WHITE HOUSE GUARD

BRITISH AMBASSADOR JAMES BRYCE

★ Prologue

NARRATOR: My name is Skip Wakefield. I am 65 years old. Back in 1880, I was part of a crew hired by the government to map the North Dakota Territory. It was then that I met Theodore Roosevelt.

★ Scene One

(A camp on the North Dakota prairie. The crew is sitting around a campfire. Joe Bayless is restless—he gets up, sits down, gets up and sits down again, nervously.)

GEORGE: What's wrong with you, Joe? You're acting like you've got a bumblebee under your saddle.

JOE: I just saw the new crew chief. And let me tell you—I'm scared.

YOUNG SKIP: Why? What's the matter with him?

JOE: Well, for one thing, he's from New York City.

TOM: New York City? You mean they sent a city slicker to lead us?

PHIL: Now, what do they know about camping and tracking out there?

JOE: And that ain't the worst of it. The durn galoot's got a big bag full of books with 'im! He's a...a...bookworm.

GEORGE: BOOKS?

JOE: Yup. With HARD COVERS, too! He's never been on a crew. Says he learned all about the great outdoors from reading about it in his books. That's probably what made his eyes so weak he has to wear those great big round glasses!

PHIL: GLASSES? Everyone knows readin's no good for your eyes. Poor soul prob'ly couldn't see a grizzly bear if it jumped up and roared in front of his face!

TOM: That book-readin' city slicker's gonna get us all killed.

(Petey and TR enter. TR is wearing a large hat and his glasses. The crew quiets down.)

PETEY: Uh, boys, this here is our new chief. Chief, this is Tom, Joe, Skip, Phil, and George.

TR: Bully to meet you, men!

CREW: *(together)* Hello, Chief.

PHIL: *(under his breath)* "Bully"? What does that mean?

TR: *(not hearing Phil)* Men, our job is to track the northwest forty square miles of this territory and report back to Washington. We will leave tomorrow at four A.M. and head for the first corner of our quadrant. Bully?

(No response. The men are confused.)

TR: Men?

(Still no response.)

TR: Do…you…understand?

CREW: Oh, yes! Yes, sir.

TR: Then it's bully! Just bully.

JOE: Excuse me, sir, but usually we would leave at five, to get the extra rest, and move off with the dawn.

YOUNG SKIP: And it's already past ten at night. That doesn't leave a lot of time to rest.

TR: Then let's get to sleep now. See you at four, men.

(TR heads off to his tent.)

JOE: Durned city slicker.

★ Scene Two

NARRATOR: The next morning we'd been on the trail for an hour when the sun started to come up.

JOE: Consarn it! I'm so darn tired I can barely see straight.

YOUNG SKIP: Hey, Petey, ask City Slicker if we can take a breather.

PETEY: All right, I'll go ask him.

(Petey goes to TR at the front of the line.)

PETEY: Excuse me, chief. The men asked if we can stop to rest.

TR: Is someone injured?

PETEY: No, sir.

TR: *(whipping out a pad of paper and reading from it)* Well, by my calculations, if we march for two and one half hours, then rest for thirty minutes, then march for another two and one-half hours, we will reach our destination by ten thirty, eat a meal, and begin our mapping. If we are to stay on schedule, then we still have one and one half hours to go before we can stop for our first rest.

PETEY: And are we on schedule?

TR: We are on schedule, and we are going to stay on schedule. But we have much to do. So no rests, not now.

PETEY: Yes, sir.

(Petey walks back to the line.)

NARRATOR: Petey explained what City Slicker had told him.

JOE: Figures. Calculations. Huh! That may be how they keep the trolleys running in New York City, but it's not going to work out here.

YOUNG SKIP: He'll have to figure that out for himself.

PETEY: Well, he has given us a half-hour rest period, and a meal at ten thirty— that's more than the last chief gave us.

JOE: Say, who's side are you on? The last chief had experience. He wasn't a city slicker with his schedules and his books and his "bully" this and "bully" that!

PETEY: No, sir!

★ Scene Three

(The crew is resting and eating. TR is off alone, writing a letter.)

TR: My dear Edith, we are out on the plains and it is beautiful. The work is hard, but it makes you feel strong. The crew are good men. I am worried, though, as these men have much more experience tracking these hills than I have. Plus, I know they still look at me as a city boy who wouldn't know a rock from a bird. I hope this does not become a problem, so we can be successful in our quest. Love, Theodore.

(At her home, Edith Carow receives TR's letter. She reads it and begins to write him back.)

EDITH: Theodore, remember what you know, and act on it. Any man can respect someone who acts out of the confidence of his knowledge, and these men are no different. They may know the trails, but you know how to lead. Don't ever forget that. Awaiting your return, Edith.

(As TR reads the last line, Petey and the crew approach.)

PETEY: Excuse me, Chief, the men were wondering where we would be heading next.

TR: Men, we will camp here for a day and map, then head north. Skip, Joe, begin unloading the equipment.

YOUNG SKIP: Yes, sir.

(TR goes back to his tent. Young Skip and Joe unload the equipment.)

JOE: Did he say north?

TOM: Yeah, what of it?

JOE: Oh, nothing, except that's Sioux territory, that's all.

TOM, PETEY, PHIL, GEORGE: Sioux! They're good fighters!

GEORGE: Maybe you should tell City Slicker this. Maybe he doesn't know it.

JOE: He's getting paid to lead us—he's supposed to know these things—'ceptin' he can't, cause he ain't never been out here before. Let him worry about the Sioux.

GEORGE: Don't fool around, Joe. If those Sioux are unfriendly, we should go another way.

JOE: Don't worry, I'm sure old City Slicker's got a book that'll tell him just what to do when you meet the Sioux. Hey, that rhymes.

(TR walks over.)

TR: What's all the discussion?

(The crew look at each other, then look at Joe.)

YOUNG SKIP: Joe has something we think you ought to know, Chief.

(All look at Joe. Joe is annoyed.)

TR: Yes, Joe?

JOE: I have nothing to say.

GEORGE: Joe thinks you're leading us right into Sioux territory.

TR: So?

PHIL: So? What if the Sioux don't want us in their territory? We don't want to have to fight them.

TR: *(laughs)* Is that what all this is about? Why, men, you're standing in Sioux territory right now.

ALL: What?

TR: We've been in the Dakotas for months and we haven't even seen a Sioux. They are nomadic— they wander over the land, following the buffalo herds. The buffalo stay away from the white settlements. So for the most part the Sioux and the whites leave each other alone.

TOM: Really?

TR: Of course. It's a well-known fact. I read it. Don't you men read books?

PHIL: Well, uh…

GEORGE: I don't like to bring my books with me on the trail, Chief—might get dirty, or…

PETEY: Yeah…anyway, who has time to read?

YOUNG SKIP: The fact is, Chief, not a lot of us can read.

TR: Is this true?

TOM: I'm afraid so, sir.

TR: This will never do. Petey, please go into my tent and fetch me my books.

> *(Petey does.)*

TR: From here on out, every meal stop, every night, we will read aloud to each other. By the end of this trip, every one of you men is going to know how to read.

> *(Petey hands out the books.)*

NARRATOR: Petey gave each one of us a book. None of us knew what to do with them, since they all had lots of pages and no pictures.

TR: Carry these with you at all times, and we will read them together. All right, men, let's get to sleep—we have an early start tomorrow!

TOM: Hmph! Thanks for the book, City Slicker.

> *(All look at Tom in shock. TR laughs.)*

TR: You can use that name if you want. But my name is Theodore. Theodore Roosevelt.

PHIL: Thanks for the book, Theodore.

TR: Bully.

NARRATOR: By the time we mapped the territory and returned, we all knew how to read. Not real well, but well enough. And we stopped calling Theodore "City Slicker." And, you know—we never did run into any Sioux.

★  *Scene Four*

NARRATOR: Years later, when our pal Theodore became President of the United States, we all decided to pay a call on him. We didn't know he was entertaining the British ambassador that day.

(The White House. TR and Edith, now Mrs. Roosevelt, are waiting at the door for the British ambassador, when another cab drives up.)

TR: Skip! Tom! So good to see you. Edith, these are the good men I worked with in Dakota Territory.

EDITH: A pleasure to meet you, gentlemen.

(George, Phil, Petey also get out.)

TR: George, Petey, Philip—and Joe! You're all looking well. You must be working hard.

JOE: Good to see you again, Mr. President.

NARRATOR: Just then, another cab pulled up to the White House.

GUARD: Ambassador James Bryce of Great Britain, sir.

(Bryce gets out of the cab, a little startled to see the crowd. TR steps forward.)

TR: Welcome to the White House, Mr. Ambassador.

BRYCE: Thank you, Mr. President.

TR: May I present our companions for lunch? These are some of the men who tracked the West with me.

BRYCE: They will be joining us for lunch?

TR: Not only joining us for lunch, but I hope they will stay afterward, so we can entertain each other by reading aloud.

BRYCE: *(skeptical but polite)* Sounds interesting. I look forward to it. A pleasure to meet you all.

YOUNG SKIP: And you, Mr. Ambassador.

TR: Bully.

BRYCE: Thank you, Mr. President.

JOE: Ah, Mr. President, there's just one thing I've always wanted to know, and I've never been able to find the answer...even in a book!

TR: And what might that be, Joe?

JOE: Just what in tarnation does *bully* mean, anyway?

(They all laugh as they go inside.)

NARRATOR: We all had a good laugh, even TR and the ambassador. You know, TR often said that if it were not for the strenuous life he had led out West, with us, he might have grown up the same weak person he was as a child—maybe even died of asthma. Yet he became a great president, and our friend. Our friend, the city slicker, President Roosevelt. Bully for him!

Theodore Roosevelt
Teacher's Guide

Biography

Theodore Roosevelt was born in New York City in 1858. Sick and weak during much of his boyhood, he suffered from asthma, which kept him from attending school, so his aunt taught him at home.

Young Theodore was an avid naturalist, collecting butterflies, dead mice, birds, frogs, and anything else he could catch.

In 1881 Roosevelt was elected to the New York State Legislature. He became known as a reformer, speaking against corrupt politicians. He soon became the leader of the Republican party in New York, and later the police commissioner of New York City. He moved to the Dakota Territory in 1884, and became a rancher. There he developed his famous barrel chest and thick neck.

During the Spanish-American War in 1898, Roosevelt commanded a group of soldiers called the Rough Riders, leading a charge up San Juan Hill that made him a national hero. He became William McKinley's running mate in 1900, vice president in 1901, and later that year became president when McKinley was assassinated. Roosevelt continued his reform platform, passed laws against monopolies, or "trusts," ended the Pennsylvania coal strike, planned and built the Panama Canal, and settled the Russo-Japanese War, for which he became the first American president to win the Nobel Prize for Peace. He stepped down after his second term, and died at his Long Island home in 1919.

Classroom Activities

★ Talk About It

The crew had a stereotyped notion of what a crew leader should be—and Theodore Roosevelt, with his books and his urban background, didn't fit the stereotype. Discuss with students how believing in stereotypes can often be limiting.

★ Write About It

Theodore Roosevelt would feel very much at ease with society's current emphasis on conservation and the environment. Yet he was also interested in hunting, and would probably not agree with the most extreme animal-rights activists. Invite interested students to research Theodore Roosevelt's beliefs about nature and the environment. When they have gathered enough information, invite students to pick three current environmental issues and write what Roosevelt's position would be on each. Encourage them to support their ideas with facts from research.

★ Report on It

Theodore Roosevelt was one of the most colorful characters to occupy the White House. Students should enjoy creating presentations based on their research into the different careers he pursued on the way to the presidency: Rough Rider, journalist, rancher, and so forth.

George Washington • John Adams • Thomas Jefferson • James Madison • James Monroe • John Quincy Adams • Andrew Jackson • Martin Van Buren • William Henry Harrison • John Tyler • James K. Polk • Zachary Taylor • Millard Fillmore • Franklin Pierce • James Buchanan • Abraham Lincoln • Andrew Johnson • Ulysses S. Grant • Rutherford B. Hayes • James A. Garfield • Chester A. Arthur • Grover Cleveland • Benjamin Harrison • Grover Cleveland • William McKinley • Theodore Roosevelt • William H. Taft • Woodrow Wilson • Warren G. Harding • Calvin Coolidge • Herbert C. Hoover • Franklin D. Roosevelt • Harry S Truman • Dwight D. Eisenhower • John F. Kennedy • Lyndon B. Johnson • Richard M. Nixon • Gerald R. Ford • James Earl Carter • Ronald Reagan • George Bush • William Jefferson Clinton

Woodrow Wilson
The Fourteen Points

CAST
NARRATOR ONE
NARRATOR TWO
WOODROW WILSON
SENATOR HENRY CABOT LODGE
SECRETARY OF STATE ROBERT LANSING
EDITH WILSON
GEORGES CLEMENCEAU
DAVID LLOYD GEORGE
VITTORIO ORLANDO

★ Scene One

NARRATOR ONE: It is January 1918. The nations of Europe have been at war for four years. England, France, and Italy, known as the Allies, have been fighting Germany in trench warfare. Conditions are terrible.

NARRATOR TWO: As America prepares to enter the war on the side of the Allies, President Woodrow Wilson tries to plan ahead—for a strategy that will bring the war to a quick end.

NARRATOR ONE: One day in 1918, Woodrow sat talking with his wife, Edith.

WOODROW: There has to be a way to keep war like this from happening ever again. Look at the causes of this war: secret agreements between nations, grudges, long-festering feuds. Why, these European nations have been fighting for so long, they can't remember what it's like to be at peace.

EDITH: Maybe they need someone from the outside to show them the way out of war…with its tanks, poison gas, men living in trenches for *years*, those airplanes dropping bombs…. Society has become so good at inventing machines for war—shouldn't we be able to invent a way to prevent war?

WOODROW: Yes, we should. I'm going to try to come up with an idea to do it.

★ Scene Two

NARRATOR TWO: Woodrow did come up with an idea. He bases a peace plan around fourteen principles that all nations could agree on. If these fourteen points are accepted, it would be the first time that all the world's nations agree on a single set of laws.

NARRATOR ONE: Woodrow presents his "Fourteen Points" speech in Washington.

WOODROW: Thank you. My fellow Americans, while we must fight this war as hard as we can win, we must see that we never engage in a world war again. In order to ensure peace, I propose the Fourteen Points. They include: No more secret treaties, freedom of the seas, free and equal trade, reduction of all armies, impartial judgement of all colonial claims, and the formation of a League of Nations. This League of Nations would be a general association of nations existing for the purpose of airing claims and settling disputes.

NARRATOR ONE: Many in Congress and government, including Woodrow's friend, Secretary of State Robert Lansing, truly believe the Fourteen Points would be a step toward a lasting peace.

NARRATOR TWO: But there are others who are not as enthusiastic. One is Senator Henry Cabot Lodge of Massachusetts.

LODGE: These Fourteen Points are dangerous ideas. We cannot enforce freedom of the seas for the whole world. And we have no business in a League of Nations! We are the United States of America. We should not be handing over decision-making power over our nation to these Europeans, who cannot even stay out of fights with each other. What do we care if the nations of Europe want to spend their time fighting each other? It shouldn't matter to us one bit—let them kill themselves, it's nothing to do with us!

LANSING: Senator Lodge, the United States, under President Wilson, has a chance to end war *forever*—how can you be against that?

LODGE: Look, I'll tell you how the United States can have peace—by minding our own business. The President of the United States is not the president of the world. He should worry only about problems at home. This war never threatened our shores. We should have stayed out of it!

LANSING: Senator, have you forgotten that Germany was trying to get Mexico to attack us? *That* certainly would have threatened our shores!

LODGE: Bah! Don't confuse the issue. I still say the Fourteen Points are dangerous.

★ Scene Three

NARRATOR TWO: Many Americans agree with Senator Lodge, but most people support the Fourteen Points.

NARRATOR ONE: Airplanes drop copies of the Fourteen Points printed in German over German cities. The German people are weary of war, and anxious for peace, but they are afraid to surrender, because they know the other nations of Europe will punish them harshly for starting the war. But after they read the Points, they have confidence that they will be treated with mercy, and agree to surrender.

NARRATOR TWO: Peace is declared on November 11, 1918, and the Allies and the Germans meet in Paris to write the peace treaty. Woodrow, Edith, and Robert Lansing all go to Paris for the peace talks.

NARRATOR ONE: From her hotel room window, Edith can see the people of Paris celebrating the end of the war.

EDITH: It's incredible, isn't it?

WOODROW: My goodness, it is. I can't believe they are all cheering—for me!

NARRATOR TWO: True, the crowds cheer for Woodrow Wilson—but when he sees the thousands of cheering people, it starts to go to his head. Woodrow begins to believe everyone supports him and his Fourteen Points.

★ Scene Four

NARRATOR ONE: Woodrow is the people's hero. And because he has the people behind him, he assumes that the leaders of the Allies are with him, too.

NARRATOR TWO: But when Woodrow arrives at the peace talks at Versailles, he and Lansing found a very different picture.

WOODROW: *(looking around the room)* I see the British, the French, the Italians. But where is the German representative?

LANSING: Sir, the other leaders made him sit out in the hall.

WOODROW: What!? What happened to treating the Germans with justice— we're getting off on the wrong foot here. *(turning to the other countries' representatives)* Gentlemen. Have you forgotten? In my Fourteen Points, it clearly states—

CLEMENCEAU: *(interrupting)* Look here, Mr. Wilson. Your Fourteen Points are all very well, but the Germans started this war, and it is the Germans who must pay for it. They must be punished! Starting by having them sit out in the hall.

ALL THE OTHER LEADERS: *(chuckling in agreement)* Hear, hear. Quite right! That's the way to handle those villains.

WOODROW: But the Germans only surrendered because the Fourteen Points promised we would not punish them or hold grudges.

CLEMENCEAU: *(looking around in mock surprise)* I made no deal. Did you, David?

LLOYD GEORGE: Not that I recall. Vittorio?

ORLANDO: No.

WILSON: But… the Fourteen Points…

CLEMENCEAU: I'm getting fed up hearing about your Fourteen Points. Walk through our land, Mr. President. Our beautiful French countryside has been destroyed. Millions of Frenchmen are dead because of German aggression. And you say "forgive them?" No. Never! Not after the suffering they've caused.

WOODROW: But we must forgive, if we want a just peace…

ORLANDO: Just? Where is the justice for Italy? You'd sing a different tune if it were the American fields that had been destroyed, and your sons and daughters killed. After all, your soldiers didn't even get here until the last year of the war.

WOODROW: *(furious)* And if they hadn't gotten here, you would still be fighting!

LLOYD GEORGE: Gentlemen, gentlemen…let's not start another war. Wilson—you want your League of Nations? You can have it—but at a price. And the price is this: the Germans must surrender the land they took in the war. The German army and navy must be destroyed. The Germans must pay my nation and the other nations heavy fines for the destruction they caused. And that's just for starters.

WOODROW: But that will destroy their economy.

LLOYD GEORGE: Well, they should have thought of that when they started the war.

ORLANDO: Yes. What's wrong with that? We suffered, now they will suffer.

WOODROW: *(looking around in dismay)* You all agree with this? *(They all nod.)* No League?

ORLANDO: No League. Unless the Germans are smashed.

WOODROW: I see. You leave me no choice. Very well, gentlemen: draw up the treaty. Call the Germans in. We'll all sign it. But mark my words: the next generation will have to undo what we're doing here today.

LANSING: Mr. Wilson, you believed in the Fourteen Points, and so did the ordinary people. But I see now that these others thought the Fourteen Points were nothing more than a lie—a trick to get the Germans to surrender. Let's just sign and get out of here.

★  Scene Five

NARRATOR TWO: Woodrow reluctantly signs the Treaty of Versailles and takes it back to Washington for ratification. According to the Constitution, all treaties the United States honors must be signed by the president and be ratified by the Senate.

NARRATOR ONE: But, just as at Versailles, Woodrow begins to have problems. He has been in Paris for six months, and that made many people angry. And as a result of his exhaustive schedule, his health is beginning to suffer.

NARRATOR TWO: And the Treaty of Versailles is running into *its* share of problems. Lansing brings the treaty to the Senate, where Senator Lodge, now the Senate leader, is waiting for him.

LODGE: Where is the president? Why isn't he here himself to discuss this?

LANSING: The president is very tired from his trip to Europe and his negotiations with the world leaders. He's resting, and he asked me to come in his place.

LODGE: Many things have changed since the president left six months ago. What the so-called "leaders of the world" have done is of no interest to me. What is of interest to me is this treaty that says we have to join this "League of Nations."

LANSING: Yes, to ensure peace.

LODGE: No! We'll ensure peace by minding our own business! We have no business in the politics of Europe—and I will not drag the United States into this.

LANSING: Senator Lodge, President Wilson did in less than two years what the European nations couldn't do in more than four years—he settled the war! We can't turn our backs on him now.

LODGE: Oh, no? You just watch.

★ Scene Six

NARRATOR ONE: In dismay, Lansing leaves the Senate and goes back to the White House. When he enters the Oval Office with Edith Wilson, he is shocked by how bad the president looks and sounds. His head droops, and his voice is gravelly and low.

WOODROW: How are you, Robert?

LANSING: Woodrow, what is the matter? You look awful.

WOODROW: Just a little fatigue, that's all. What did Lodge say?

LANSING: He's not sending the treaty for ratification.

WOODROW: I knew he wouldn't. Well, Robert, this is a democracy. One man can't impose his will on the people. Neither Lodge nor I can. Let's present the treaty to the American people, and if they decide that they don't want it, then I will accept their judgment. But I have faith in the American people. When they hear what the Fourteen Points are all about, they will support the treaty, and the League of Nations. I guarantee it. Edith, let's prepare for our trip.

EDITH: *(reluctanty)* Well… all right. But I hope your health will stand it.

★ Scene Seven

NARRATOR TWO: The president visits twenty-nine cities in only three weeks.

NARRATOR ONE: Then on a stop in Pueblo, Colorado, tragedy strikes.

EDITH: Ladies and gentlemen, one of the greatest peacemakers of our time, my husband, the President of the United States!

(The crowd cheers wildly. Woodrow steps out onto the platform.)

WOODROW: Thank you, my fellow Americans. When we were forced to enter the great conflict of war, we went in to make the world safe for democracy. The best way to make the world safe is to join the League of Nations. But there are some in Congress who think we should put our heads in the sand and forget why we fought this war, why good men died. Write your senators. Tell them that you want America to join the League of Nations! Make your decision and tell your senators what you want. Thank you, thank you all.

NARRATOR TWO: The crowd cheers wildly. But as Woodrow steps away, he falls to the ground.

NARRATOR ONE: Woodrow suffers a stroke, brought on by stress and exhaustion. He is unable to speak or get up.

★ Scene Eight

NARRATOR TWO: Edith rushes him back to Washington, but the battle for the treaty was lost.

NARRATOR ONE: Edith becomes the president's eyes, ears, and voice. She reads the newspapers and the important congressional bills to him, and only lets certain people see him, since he still looks so ill. One day, Lansing comes to visit.

WOODROW: Always good to see you, Robert. Have we joined the League?

LANSING: No, sir.

WOODROW: Then my prediction will come true. Our allies have made Germany pay so much and give so much land, the German people are full of hatred. As soon as they can, they will seek revenge. They'll strike back one day…and the cycle of war will begin again.

LANSING: Rest now, Woodrow.

NARRATOR TWO: Robert and Edith leave the room and speak outside.

EDITH: His heart is broken.

LANSING: No matter what Lodge and his supporters say, Woodrow Wilson is a great man.

NARRATOR ONE: Woodrow Wilson dies in 1924. The U.S. Senate never ratifies the Treaty of Versailles, and signs a separate peace treaty with Germany. America never joins the League of Nations.

NARRATOR TWO: And Woodrow's prediction comes true. The German people, penniless from war fines, broken in spirit, desperate for revenge, fall in behind a leader who inspires their patriotism and vows revenge on the other nations of Europe. His name is Adolf Hitler, and he starts the war that Woodrow predicted, World War II, in 1939, just twenty years after Woodrow won the Nobel Peace Prize.

Woodrow Wilson
Teacher's Guide

Biography

Woodrow Wilson was born in Stanton, Virginia, on December 29, 1856. When he was four years old, his family moved to Georgia, where they lived during the Civil War. Woodrow later pursued a career in academics, getting advanced degrees and eventually being named the President of Princeton University. As a Progressive, Wilson was nominated to run as a Democrat against the incumbent President, William Howard Taft, and former President Theodore Roosevelt, running as an independent, and was elected President in 1912. As President, Wilson lowered tariffs, established the income tax, supported women's suffrage, and oversaw the establishment of the Federal Reserve System. When World War I broke out in 1914 Wilson proclaimed the United States neutral and was able to keep the nation out of war despite aggressive German actions like the sinking of American and Allied ships by German U-Boats. The Zimmerman letter of 1917 eventually led to America's entry into the war. Wilson saw America's entry as an opportunity for lasting peace and wrote the Fourteen Points in 1918. He spent six months in Europe in 1919 negotiating the Treaty of Versailles, which ended the war and established the League of Nations. But the Treaty was rejected by the American Senate. Campaigning for its passage, Wilson suffered a stroke in 1920 and despite his enduring popularity, he was unable to run for a third term. He died on February 3, 1924.

Classroom Activities

★ Talk About It

Many of the issues Wilson and Lodge differed on are still timely today, as some Americans feel we are the last superpower and as such must assume a leadership role in world affairs, whether as peacekeepers or as soldiers. Others believe, like Lodge, that we should "mind our own business" instead of becoming involved in the internal affairs of other nations. Invite students to think about and debate their positions on this issue. Possible discussion questions are: Who do you agree with, Wilson or Lodge? Are international affairs any of our business? If so, why? If not, why not? Should a president be more concerned with international affairs or internal affairs? Support your opinion with facts from history or current events.

★ Report About It

Students can prepare for their debate by looking in the international news section of their local newspapers. There are areas of the world where the U.S. is usually likely to be involved, such as the Middle East. Other areas of recent involvement include Northern Ireland, Bosnia, and certain African nations, and the local library should have stories about these locales on file for students to research.

Some students may be interested in Wilson's prediction that the punitive Treaty of Versailles would lead to future wars. Invite them to research the causes of World War II and form an opinion as to whether Wilson was right. Did the harsh terms of that treaty contribute to the root causes of World War II?

★ Write About It

Students may want to prepare presentations on their research or write essays giving their opinions on the issues mentioned above.

As an alternative writing activity, invite students to prepare their own Fourteen Points to prevent war.

George Washington • John Adams • Thomas Jefferson • James Madison • James Monroe • John Quincy Adams • Andrew Jackson • Martin Van Buren • William Henry Harrison • John Tyler • James K. Polk • Zachary Taylor • Millard Fillmore • Franklin Pierce • James Buchanan • Abraham Lincoln • Andrew Johnson • Ulysses S. Grant • Rutherford B. Hayes • James A. Garfield • Chester A. Arthur • Grover Cleveland • Benjamin Harrison • Grover Cleveland • William McKinley • Theodore Roosevelt • William H. Taft • Woodrow Wilson • Warren G. Harding • Calvin Coolidge • Herbert C. Hoover • Franklin D. Roosevelt • Harry S Truman • Dwight D. Eisenhower • John F. Kennedy • Lyndon B. Johnson • Richard M. Nixon • Gerald R. Ford • James Earl Carter • Ronald Reagan • George Bush • William Jefferson Clinton

Franklin Delano Roosevelt

Through Tragedy to Triumph

CAST

NARRATOR ONE

NARRATOR TWO

FRANKLIN DELANO ROOSEVELT

ELEANOR ROOSEVELT

SARA DELANO ROOSEVELT

DR. WESTON

LOUIS MCHENRY HOWE

★ Scene One

(The Roosevelt's summer house on Campobello Island, Canada.)

NARRATOR ONE: Franklin Delano Roosevelt was born into wealth. His uncle, Theodore Roosevelt, had been President of the United States. But though he was rich, he had sympathy for the problems of working men and women. Working as a lawyer, he took on small-claims cases for working people, and charged them no fee. This raised his awareness of what laborers went through every day.

NARRATOR TWO: Franklin took this awareness into his political career, and people responded by voting for him. He won a seat in the New York state senate by uniting voters and laborers behind him. He soon drew the attention of Democratic party leaders. Franklin became a national political figure, and party leaders encouraged him to run for president in the following election. Life seemed to be going along beautifully for Franklin Delano Roosevelt.

NARRATOR ONE: Needing a rest from the 1920 state senate campaign, Franklin, his wife Eleanor, and his mother, Sara Delano Roosevelt, go to the Roosevelt's summer house on Campobello Island.

NARRATOR TWO: At poolside, Eleanor and her mother-in-law, Sara, read silently. Franklin swims up to them.

FRANKLIN: Enjoying the sun, dear?

ELEANOR: Yes, it's nice to rest, finally.

SARA: *(talking to her son as if he's a little boy)* Why don't you rest, Franklin?

FRANKLIN: I am resting. Swimming is very relaxing.

SARA: But Franklin—

ELEANOR: *(interrupting)* That's right, Franklin, keep it up; it's good for you!

NARRATOR ONE: Franklin swims off.

SARA: *(angry at Eleanor)* Must you always encourage him like that?

ELEANOR: He's an adult. He can do what he wants.

SARA: Well…

FRANKLIN: *(from the pool)* Help! Eleanor! Help!

ELEANOR: *(leaping up)* Franklin, what's wrong?

FRANKLIN: My legs! I can't feel anything in my—

SARA: You see. What did I tell you? He's going under. He'll drown!

ELEANOR: Hold on, Franklin. I'll get you!

NARRATOR TWO: Eleanor and the servants pulled Franklin from the pool. He had fainted. Without the rescue, he would have drowned.

NARRATOR ONE: But his problems were just beginning.

★ Scene Two

(That night at the Campobello house. Eleanor and Sara wait outside Franklin's room.)

NARRATOR TWO: Dr. Weston, a local physician, diagnoses Franklin with polio, a disease that causes some of the nerves in the body to stop working.

NARRATOR ONE: This is why Franklin lost the feeling in his legs. And the power to use them.

DR. WESTON: Mrs. Roosevelt, I'm afraid your husband has been stricken with infantile paralysis—polio.

ELEANOR: Will he live?

DR. WESTON: We can save his life, but he may have lost the use of his legs...permanently.

SARA: Oh, this is terrible.

DR. WESTON: I've called for an ambulance. We should get him to the hospital right away.

ELEANOR: Yes, Doctor, of course.

★ Scene Three

(The Roosevelt house in Hyde Park, New York)

NARRATOR TWO: Eleanor and Sara take Franklin back to the family home at Hyde Park. His close friend Louis McHenry Pike visits Franklin often.

NARRATOR ONE: The polio not only leaves Franklin unable to walk, but very depressed as well. Eleanor and Louis do their best to keep his spirits up. Sara tries to help, too, in her own way.

LOUIS: Franklin, I saw your friends from the New York State Legislature the other day. They all said hello.

FRANKLIN: *(quietly)* That's nice.

ELEANOR: Er, um, Louis was telling me they still remember that time you told that new senator that the ladies' room was the men's room. What a laugh we all had...do you remember that, Franklin?

FRANKLIN: *(mumbling)* Yes.

LOUIS: Anyway, all the boys say they can't wait to see you again, Franklin.

SARA: Well, that will have to wait. I'm afraid my Franklin won't be doing any traveling for a little while.

LOUIS: The Franklin Roosevelt I know is not one who would let something like this stop him from doing what he loves.

SARA: Eleanor, would you please step outside for a moment?

ELEANOR: Of course.

SARA: *(closing the door)* Please tell your friend to stop this talk of Franklin returning to politics at once.

ELEANOR: I will not! He's trying to keep Franklin's spirits up.

SARA: They'll only fall that much farther when he realizes he'll never get out of that bed.

ELEANOR: He will get out. Polio is just a challenge he needs to overcome. It doesn't mean he needs to become bedridden. And the sooner he gets back to work, the sooner he'll get better.

SARA: He doesn't need to work. We have wealth enough so he never has to work another day in his life. He can just live here with me and the staff to wait on him. That's the best thing to do in this little...situation. Better than filling his head with foolish notions.

ELEANOR: The only foolish notion is that he has to live as a prisoner. A prisoner of this house, of this disease, of YOU!

FRANKLIN: *(from inside)* Mother—Eleanor—stop arguing!

NARRATOR TWO: Sara and Eleanor run back into Franklin's room.

ELEANOR: You heard us?

FRANKLIN: Of course. Mother, I know you want me to stay here, where you can watch over me and take care of me. But I'm not ten years old anymore. I don't need looking after every second.

SARA: I was only trying to help…but if my help isn't wanted, I'll leave.

(She leaves the room, with Louis.)

ELEANOR: She means well.

FRANKLIN: I'll make up with her later. You know, Eleanor, I was lying here thinking about Uncle Theodore. I remember him telling me about how he was sick and weak as a child. But he never looked sick and weak to me.

ELEANOR: When I was little, I always thought he was the biggest, strongest man in the world.

FRANKLIN: He had asthma, his eyes were weak, and there were plenty of other problems he could have given in to, but he didn't.

ELEANOR: That's true. He never gave in.

FRANKLIN: No, sir. Going out to work on the ranch, mapping the wilderness, roping and riding in the great outdoors. Look what it did for him! Uncle Theodore believed all people are meant for greatness, but that we have to pursue it. And that's what I have to do. Somehow, I have to get up and run after it. With or without these legs, I have to do it! Eleanor, help me get into that wheelchair.

ELEANOR: Of course, dear, of course.

NARRATOR ONE: Eleanor helped Franklin into his chair. It was very difficult for her, since not only were his legs useless, but the muscles in his waist and hips that would normally help him walk were in great pain. But she, too, was determined.

NARRATOR TWO: When Franklin was firmly in his chair, Eleanor wheeled him out to Sara and Louis.

SARA: Eleanor! Are you trying to kill him? Franklin—get back into bed, where you belong!

FRANKLIN: *(wheeling himself over to Sara, taking her hand, and kissing it)* Mother, you're a peach. But I've had enough of lying in bed. I could use some fresh air. Come outside with me, Louis. There are a couple of upcoming campaigns that I want to talk to you about.

LOUIS: Of course, Franklin, right away.

★ Scene Four

NARRATOR ONE: And so Franklin began his comeback from polio to politics. But it was very difficult.

NARRATOR TWO: In 1928, ideas about physically challenged people were very different. Many people thought having a disability meant that a person wasn't capable of very much. Some even felt the way Sara did, that a man in a wheelchair was unfit for public office. A few even thought a person in a wheelchair wasn't fit to be even *seen* in public!

NARRATOR ONE: People knew Franklin had polio. It was a terrible disease that killed and disabled thousands of Americans in those days. But Franklin, with Eleanor's help, allowed people to think he was fully recovered. In truth, he had regained the use of some of the muscles that polio had taken away, but his legs were still paralyzed. Yet, in 1924, Franklin returned to politics, delivering a speech at the Democratic Convention that made most observers forget he'd ever been sick. And in 1928, he ran for governor of New York, and won.

NARRATOR TWO: Franklin ran a vigorous campaign, traveling all over New York State. Most people still never knew he was handicapped, because of the way Eleanor helped him. After every speech, Eleanor would stand behind Franklin and, when she was sure they couldn't be seen, wheel him off the stage and help him into his car. They would then drive through the town to meet the people. He'd sit in the car and wave. No one had to know he couldn't get up without help.

NARRATOR ONE: When he became president, Franklin never allowed himself to be photographed in the wheelchair, for fear it would make him look weak.

NARRATOR TWO: And no matter where he went, Eleanor and Louis were with him—all the way to the Oval Office.

LOUIS: Well, Franklin, you've made it to the White House—just like your Uncle Teddy.

FRANKLIN: I can hardly believe it myself, Louis. And I couldn't have been elected without you two—especially you, Eleanor. And I'll never forget how much I owe you.

ELEANOR: Franklin, it was you who never gave up. No matter how you suffered. I was happy to help.

FRANKLIN: Well, maybe my experience has had a purpose. With the country suffering these terrible economic times, I think I understand more than ever the problems of the working man and woman. I can't help but feel for them. And I want to use my presidency to help them—to make their lives better.

ELEANOR: I'm so glad to hear you say that, Franklin. So many Americans have lost their life savings, their homes, their farms, and their jobs—factories have closed, children are going hungry—it breaks my heart to see their suffering. Now that you're president, you have the power to help.

FRANKLIN: Eleanor, I know how kindhearted you are, and I promise—just as you helped me, I'll help the American people. And that's all it'll take— just a helping hand. They'll do the rest!

NARRATOR ONE: Franklin D. Roosevelt did help the American people out of the Great Depression. His administration put people back to work, building dams, bridges, roads, and more.

NARRATOR TWO: And he did it all from his wheelchair. Though the American people never knew it, the fact is, the man elected president more times than any other was also the first physically challenged American to become president.

Franklin Delano Roosevelt
Teacher's Guide

Biography

Franklin Delano Roosevelt was born on January 30, 1882, into a wealthy family. He attended private schools, went to Harvard, then to Columbia Law School before joining a law practice. Although rich, he became very concerned with the plight of the poor and working classes. He was a state senator in New York State in 1910, assistant secretary of the Navy during World War I, and a vice-presidential candidate in 1920. But in 1921 his political career was stopped by polio, and he lost the use of his legs. Yet he was elected governor of New York in 1928, and was reelected in 1930. In 1932 Roosevelt was elected to the first of four terms as president. He is the only person to win the presidency that many times.

When he took office, the nation was mired in the Depression, and he rallied the country around the New Deal, a series of programs funded by the government to put people to work. By doing this, he greatly expanded the role of the federal government. In 1941 the Japanese attacked Pearl Harbor Naval Base in Hawaii, plunging the United States into World War II. Working with British Prime Minister Winston Churchill and Russian Premier Joseph Stalin, Roosevelt devised a strategy that led to the defeat of the Axis Powers.

Having led the nation through two of its greatest crises, and having just won a fourth term in 1944, Roosevelt, exhausted, went on vacation to Warm Springs, Georgia. There, on April 12, 1945, Franklin Roosevelt died of a brain hemorrhage.

Classroom Activities

★ Talk About It

Today we say "physically challenged" or "differently abled;" not "handicapped" or "disabled." Special parking spots, access ramps, rest rooms, and "kneeling" buses show how institutions now try to include all people. So it may be difficult for students to imagine the situation in Roosevelt's day. They may not understand the need the Roosevelts felt to fool the American public about the extent of the president's condition. Encourage students to discuss whether or not it was wrong, based on the attitudes at the time, for the Roosevelts to hide Franklin's disablity.

★ Write About It

Many of the programs Roosevelt instituted, like Social Security, which were once credited with saving the country, are now decried as having made government too big. After students have learned about Roosevelt's New Deal, invite them to write essays in favor of either that caretaker role of big government, or the more limited role of government many people today call for.

★ Report on It

As mentioned in the play, FDR never allowed photos of himself in the wheelchair to be published. Given today's media scrutiny, do students think it would be possible for any candidate or president to control the media to such an extent? Suggest that interested students visit the library to compare news coverage then and now, and to present their findings.

George Washington • John Adams • Thomas Jefferson • James Madison • James Monroe • John Quincy Adams • Andrew Jackson • Martin Van Buren • William Henry Harrison • John Tyler • James K. Polk • Zachary Taylor • Millard Fillmore • Franklin Pierce • James Buchanan • Abraham Lincoln • Andrew Johnson • Ulysses S. Grant • Rutherford B. Hayes • James A. Garfield • Chester A. Arthur • Grover Cleveland • Benjamin Harrison • Grover Cleveland • William McKinley • Theodore Roosevelt • William H. Taft • Woodrow Wilson • Warren G. Harding • Calvin Coolidge • Herbert C. Hoover • Franklin D. Roosevelt • Harry S. Truman • Dwight D. Eisenhower • John F. Kennedy • Lyndon B. Johnson • Richard M. Nixon • Gerald R. Ford • James Earl Carter • Ronald Reagan • George Bush • William Jefferson Clinton

Dwight David Eisenhower

The Supreme Commander

CAST

NARRATOR ONE

NARRATOR TWO

PRESIDENT FRANKLIN ROOSEVELT

GENERAL GEORGE MARSHALL

GENERAL GEORGE S. PATTON

GENERAL OMAR BRADLEY

GENERAL GEORGE MONTGOMERY

GENERAL DWIGHT D. EISENHOWER (IKE)

AL, EISENHOWER'S AIDE

SOLDIER

RADIO OPERATOR

MAMIE EISENHOWER

★ Scene One

NARRATOR ONE: World War II had been raging for some time, and with America finally in the battle, there was a glimmer of hope for the Allies. With the Allied armies driving the Nazis out of Africa and marching north through Italy and Greece, their three leaders—President Franklin Roosevelt, Prime Minister Winston Churchill of Great Britain, and Joseph Stalin, Premier of the Soviet Union—met to plan their next moves.

NARRATOR TWO: They decided that to win the war they would have to invade France with a massive army. The invasion of France became known as D-Day.

(In the Oval Office, President Roosevelt sits behind his desk. General Marshall walks in.)

ROOSEVELT: George, I'll get right down to the problem. I know Eisenhower and the rest of his officers are expecting you to go to Europe to lead the invasion of France. But George, I cannot spare you from here. I want General Eisenhower to lead the invasion. I am going to name him Supreme Commander of the Allied Forces. Churchill and Stalin have agreed. Do you think he is up to the task?

MARSHALL: Mr. President, I think the only man who can keep the Alliance together through such a massive undertaking is Ike. The other generals respect him, and the men love him. He's our only hope of success.

ROOSEVELT: I'm glad to hear you say that. I will notify him immediately.

(Marshall leaves.)

NARRATOR ONE: General Marshall cables England to inform Eisenhower that he has been named supreme commander. But when Ike (as everyone calls him) receives the news, he is actually more troubled than excited. This is going to be a terribly difficult operation.

NARRATOR TWO: Five different invasion forces are going to cross the English Channel. The Nazis have many men waiting on the French side. The tides are difficult and there are often storms on the channel. On top of that, there is an ongoing feud between England's Bernard Montgomery and America's George Patton, two of the Allied generals. But Ike knows the invasion of France is the last best hope for defeating the Nazis. The pressure is on. Ike met with his generals: George Patton and Omar Bradley (he and Ike had been friends at West Point), and Bernard Montgomery. On the other side of the English Channel, the Nazi army waited under the command of their great general, Erwin Rommel.

★ Scene Two

(Allied Supreme Headquarters, in the south of England. Eisenhower, Bradley, Montgomery, Patton, and their aides stand around a large table looking at maps of the English Channel and France.)

PATTON: Erwin Rommel is the best general the Nazis have. I've studied every move he's made. He's crafty. He does things that you would think are insane, but they work. Like moving his entire army in the middle of the night. You wake up , the army's gone. You turn around to get a cup of coffee, and there he is, in line with you.

BRADLEY: With half of the German army.

PATTON: Exactly. He knows us as well as we know us. What we can do is surprise him. A full frontal assault, with all our tanks and men, will be the last thing he's expecting.

MONTGOMERY: That's insane. We'll lose all our tanks and many men will die.

PATTON: Not as many men as will die if we fight a conventional battle against Rommel's best.

MONTGOMERY: You do what you think you have to do. I will not send my men into such an insane affair.

PATTON: Then your men better learn how to speak German!

MONTGOMERY. What do you know? Have you ever fought Rommel? I have!

PATTON: Yes, and you lost, badly!

MONTGOMERY: Why you...

BRADLEY: Now, gentlemen...

EISENHOWER: All right then, the American forces will attack here, on these two beaches. The British forces will attack on these two, the Canadians on this one. The paratroopers will be the first ones in, and block any escape route for the Nazis. The battleships will stand offshore and shell Nazi positions, making it as clear as possible for our soldiers. Monty, you will be directing the British forces on these two beaches. George, you will take the larger invasion force of Americans. Omar, you will take the other one. Are there any questions? *(None reply.)* Good, then we will wait on the tide and weather reports and the moon. If the moon is too bright our position will be given away. If the weather is too rough and the tides too high, we will lose our armies before we even get to the beaches. So we'll wait until we hear those reports. Until then, that's all, gentlemen. *(The generals start to leave.)* General Bradley, will you wait a minute?

(Bradley stays. Patton and Montgomery leave.)

EISENHOWER: Omar, tell me the truth. Do you think George was right?

BRADLEY: I think you were right, Ike.

EISENHOWER: That's not what I asked you.

BRADLEY: Rommel has been beating Montgomery for months. He's got nothing left. Of course he's going to be cautious. George, on the other hand, has been dying to mix it up with Rommel. I think you met them both in the middle, and you did the right thing.

EISENHOWER: The one thing I know is that Hitler would love it if we started fighting him separately. His forces are stronger than any one of our armies. The only way we can save the world from the Nazis is to work together.

NARRATOR ONE: Bradley leaves and Al, Eisenhower's aide. enters.

EISENHOWER: Any word yet?

AL: None, General.

EISENHOWER: I'm going to take a walk.

NARRATOR TWO: As he walks around the camp, Ike sees the thousands and thousands of soldiers preparing their rifles and gear for the upcoming battle. He stops in front of one. When the solider sees the supreme commander standing in front of him, he drops his gear, salutes, and stands at attention

SOLDIER: Ten-hut.

EISENHOWER: At ease. You must be surprised to see me here. *(The soldier finishes his salute.)* How are you tonight, soldier? Are you ready to go?

SOLIDER: *(nervously)* Y-Yes, sir.

EISENHOWER: Don't be nervous, son. You know, many people think it's the generals that win wars, but it's men like you, the toughest, most noble fighters in the world who are going to win it. You men are my heroes. *(He gives the soldier a big smile.)* You like football, soldier?

SOLDIER: Yes, sir!

EISENHOWER: I used to play football at West Point. Do you know what our coach use to say every year before we played Navy?

SOLDIER: What was that, sir?

EISENHOWER: He would say, "Let's show them what the best in the world can do. Let's show them why we're the best." Do you think you're the best, soldier?

SOLDIER: Yessir!!

EISENHOWER: That's fine, soldier. Goodnight.

NARRATOR ONE: Later that night, Ike is in his study when Al, his aide, comes in with the weather report.

AL: General, this report just came in.

(Eisenhower takes the report. He hands Al a note.)

EISENHOWER: Al, I want you to take this note. If anything goes wrong tomorrow, read this to the press.

(Al takes the note and reads it.)

AL: "We have fought hard against a difficult and well-trained enemy, and in the end, our forces did not prevail and we were beaten back. The blame for this terrible defeat is mine and mine alone. General Dwight Eisenhower." Sir, I don't understand.

EISENHOWER: Got to be ready for anything. And I want it clear that if we fail, it is my fault. That's what comes with being in charge. Do you understand?

AL: Yes, sir.

EISENHOWER: Under no circumstances are you to publicize that note until I tell you to.

AL: Yes, sir. Good night, sir.

★ Scene Three

NARRATOR TWO: On the morning of June 6, 1944, the largest invasion in world history begins. The armies of the United States, Great Britain, and Canada invades the north coast of France. They face the powerful Nazi army head on. Paratroopers land behind enemy lines in the middle of the night, battleships line the coast and begin shelling before dawn, and, finally, troops begin wading ashore through the Channel tides up to the French beaches. But the invasion does not go entirely as planned.

NARRATOR ONE: The paratroopers miss their targets and end up lost in the French countryside, unable to help much. Despite the weather report, it is rainy and stormy on the morning of June 6, and some of the battleships are unable to aim their guns correctly. The seas are so stormy that some men are lost in the water before they ever get to the shore. And when the armies do land on the shore, the Nazis are waiting for them.

(Eisenhower, in his headquarters, stands over a table listening to radio reports of the invasion.)

RADIO OPERATOR: General?

EISENHOWER: Yes?

RADIO OPERATOR: The American Third Army has established a hold on the beach.

EISENHOWER: That's Patton's group. Good.

RADIO OPERATOR: The next wave of men and supplies are moving onto the beach. The Germans are beginning to retreat!

(A cheer goes up from the room. Eisenhower smiles.)

NARRATOR TWO: The first troops to hit the beach are nearly all wiped out. But by the end of the day, the Allies establish a beachhead and drive the Germans back. The invasion holds, but at the cost of many thousands of soldiers.

EISENHOWER: Begin preparing to move headquarters to the north of France.

★ *Scene Four*

NARRATOR ONE: Ike sets up new headquarters in the northern town of St. Lo, France. As he prepares his desk, Al comes in.

AL: General, reports from Patton and Montgomery say that the Germans have been captured at Caen, and that they expect our troops to begin the march into Paris any day now.

EISENHOWER: Very good.

AL: And I have a message from General Marshall, sir. May I read it?

EISENHOWER: Yes, of course.

AL: "Ike—Hear you are in France now. Hear it is a beautiful country. Invasion is a success. Good job. Marshall."

EISENHOWER: Thank you. That makes me feel good.

AL: There is also a letter from your wife, sir. I will leave that with you.

EISENHOWER: Thank you, Al.

NARRATOR TWO: When Al pulls out the letter, he also finds the note Eisenhower had given him the night before the invasion. With a smile on his face, he hands it to Ike.

EISENHOWER: What's this?

AL: The note you wrote the night before D-Day, in case everything failed. You still want it?

EISENHOWER: Sure.

NARRATOR ONE: Ike looks the note over, then crinkles it up and throws it away. He then reads his wife Mamie's letter.

MAMIE: Dear Ike: I am so proud of you. You have led the free world's armies against the evil of the Nazis. You held the different armies and leaders together, and gave the soldiers in the front lines confidence to fight and win. You are a not only a hero but a true leader.

NARRATOR TWO: Within a year after the D-Day invasion, the Nazis surrender to the Allies, and Ike is hailed as a hero around the world. It is this heroism that carries him to the presidency just seven years later. Ike never forgets the common man, the laborer, the soldier, the men and women who work hard and without fanfare to keep the country moving.

Dwight David Eisenhower
Teacher's Guide

Biography

Dwight D. Eisenhower was born on October 14, 1890, in Denison, Texas. When still a child, his family moved to Abilene, Kansas. His family was poor and Dwight and his five brothers were often teased because they wore hand-me-down shoes and tattered clothing. When Dwight was 18 he entered West Point, the United States Military Academy, to get a free education—the only kind he could afford.

After graduating, Eisenhower decided on a military career and requested an overseas assignment during World War I. However, his ability to work with young soldiers was immediately recognized and he was ordered to stay stateside to train recruits. Eisenhower led the invasions of North Africa, Sicily, and Italy before President Roosevelt named him supreme commander of the D-Day invasion. After the war Eisenhower remained in Paris and oversaw Europe's transition to peacetime.

In 1948 Eisenhower turned down the Democrats' request to run for president, but he ran and won as a Republican in 1952. As president, Eisenhower oversaw the end of the Korean War and the downfall of Senator Joseph McCarthy's Communist witch hunts. He also guided the country through some of the roughest days of the Cold War. Eisenhower suffered a heart attack in 1954, but ran and won reelection in 1956. Eisenhower died at his Gettysburg home on March 28, 1969.

Classroom Activities

★ Talk About It

Eisenhower was beloved as a good man and a war hero which made his election to president easier. Today few candidates for office have a similar war record to point to, and if they do, few citizens seem to find it very important. Invite students to discuss the importance they attach to military service in assessing a candidate's fitness to govern a nation in peacetime. Are the discipline and leadership skills learned in the military good preparation for leading a country? Or do they think other qualities are equally important?

★ Write About It

The 1950s were often called the "Eisenhower Era," and many students may have aunts, uncles, parents, or grandparents who grew up during those days. Students may enjoy researching popular culture of the '50s, perhaps by conducting interviews with family members or friends to discover how styles, education, music, and other aspects of American life were different then. Students can then write about what they've learned, or share the interviews with classmates.

There is a famous photograph of General Eisenhower talking with a paratrooper on the day before D-Day. If possible, have your librarian find it in a resource book and show this photograph to students as they read Scene Three. Then have them assume the role of the soldier and write what his role in the invasion is, what he thinks of General Eisenhower, and why he is part of the invasion.

★ Report on It

Invite students to present their research in any of the following forms: a compare and contrast chart; a video interview; a team presentation, with each member reporting on some aspect of the Eisenhower Era; a '50s fashion show, a learning wall, or an informal presentation by a family member who wants to share memories.

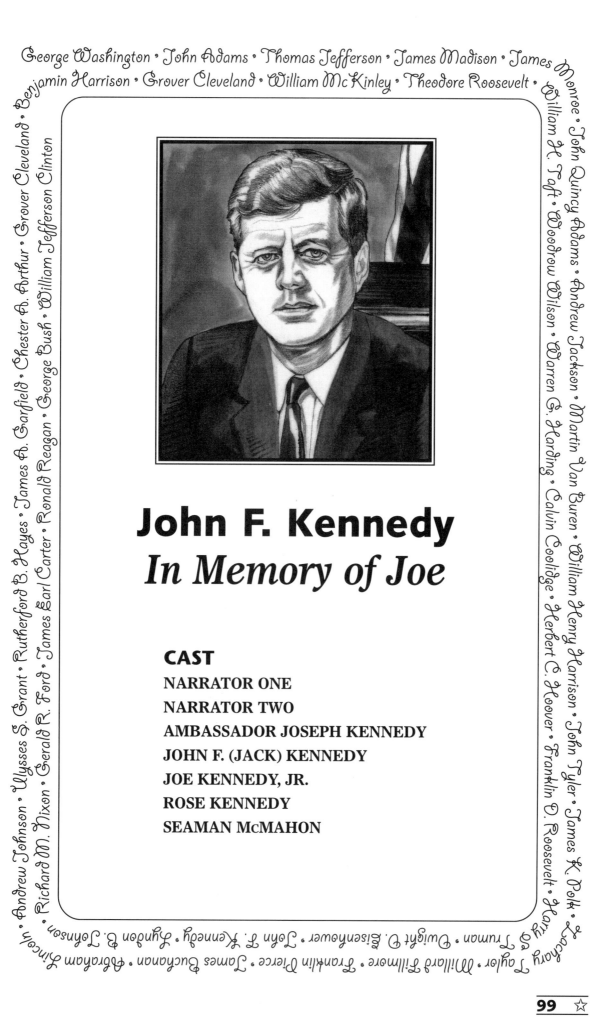

John F. Kennedy
In Memory of Joe

CAST

NARRATOR ONE

NARRATOR TWO

AMBASSADOR JOSEPH KENNEDY

JOHN F. (JACK) KENNEDY

JOE KENNEDY, JR.

ROSE KENNEDY

SEAMAN McMAHON

★ Prologue

NARRATOR ONE: 1938. A large, old house in London where the Kennedy family lives while father Joe Kennedy serves as the American ambassador to Great Britain. It is John F. (Jack) Kennedy's 21st birthday. Jack is a fun-loving young man, not a very good student, whose health is marred by Addison's disease and back troubles. Nevertheless, he is a good-natured son and brother.

NARRATOR TWO: When John Fitzgerald Kennedy turned 21, his father was the Ambassador to Britain. Ambassador Kennedy was a very rich and powerful man. He was friends with the President of the United States, the Prime Minister of Great Britain, and the King.

NARRATOR ONE: Ambassador Kennedy had definite ideas about his family, and definite plans for his first son, his namesake, Joe Kennedy, Jr. He wanted Joe, Jr. to become the first Irish Catholic president of the United States. He thought Jack would become a professor or an author. But Joe, Jr. was his pride and joy.

AMBASSADOR KENNEDY: Jack, you are twenty-one today. Congratulations. Today you are a man. And so you are entitled to the trust fund your mother and I started for you when you were a baby. One million dollars. Use it wisely.

JACK: Thank you, Mom and Dad. You have both been very generous with me. I hope I can repay you by being the best person I can be, and making you both proud, like Joe, here.

(The family applauds. A servant dishes out the cake. As everyone eats, Joe turns to Jack.)

JOE: Nice speech, brother. So, what is it you want to be best at?

JACK: Joe, I haven't the slightest idea. You have it easy—Dad's got your whole life planned out for you: a career in the military, the Senate, and then president! All you have to do is follow Dad's plan.

JOE: Don't worry, Jack. You'll do okay. Eat your cake. Oh, and by the way…it's not so easy as you think, following Dad's plan.

★ Scene One

(Two years later. Ambassador Kennedy is in his office, speaking angrily into the phone as Joe enters.)

AMBASSADOR KENNEDY: I don't care what you want! *(He slams down the receiver.)* Huh! That was the prime minister on the phone! He says if the Nazis invade Poland, he's going to declare war! I tried to reason with him, but he wouldn't listen to me. Joe, I'm sending you back to the States, where you'll be safe.

JOE: Just a minute, Dad. You seem to be forgetting I'm in the Army Air Corps. I can't just get up and go wherever I want.

AMBASSADOR KENNEDY: *You* seem to be forgetting who you're talking to. I've already put in the call to President Roosevelt. He's transferring you to an army office in Washington, D.C. Someplace where you'll be safe.

JOE: That's unfair to the other men in my unit, Dad. They don't have a wealthy father to pull strings for them.

AMBASSADOR KENNEDY: You'll thank me when they've all been blown to bits and you're in the White House. Now I won't hear any more arguments on this topic. You're going back to the States, and that's that! I won't have my plans for your future spoiled by Hitler or Churchill, and certainly not by your idealistic rumblings about what's fair.

(Before Joe can reply, Jack enters.)

AMBASSADOR KENNEDY: What is it, Jack?

JACK: Er, I just wanted to tell you, Dad…I've decided to try going back to school.

AMBASSADOR KENNEDY: So, Jack, where is it this time?

JACK: Er, Harvard.

AMBASSADOR KENNEDY: Well, I hope you do better there than you did at that other place. What was it, Princeton?

JACK: Yes, Dad.

AMBASSADOR KENNEDY: Well, I have work to do. Jack, if you need money for tuition, fine. Now, if you will excuse me I'm rather busy.

NARRATOR TWO: Ambassador Kennedy went back to work. Jack left, dejected. Outside his father's office, Jack saw his mother, Rose.

ROSE: What's the matter, son?

JACK: I wanted to talk to Dad about going back to school, but he sent me away.

ROSE: Jack, don't forget, he's got a lot on his mind. These are terrible times right now. What did you want to talk to him about? Maybe I can help.

JACK: It's just that Dad always seems to know just what he wants and how to get it. Joe, too. Me, no matter what happens, it doesn't seem to work out. I know I'm not a very good student. All I can do is swim, and that's only because I've had to swim so much to exercise my bad back.

ROSE: Jack, I know your father is gruff, but he loves you. You and your brothers and sisters have much, much, more than most young people your age. With all that you have comes great responsibility. The thing for you to do is learn to use your wealth and position wisely. Help others. There are many ways to do that. Become a lawer, a doctor, a teacher, an author. And remember: You're lucky to be an American—that means you can be anything you want.

JACK: Thanks, Mom. You always make me feel better.

NARRATOR ONE: The Nazis invade Poland, and Britain and France go to war with Germany. World War II begins. Joe, Jr. goes to Washington, as his father wants. And Jack goes back to school.

★ Scene Two

NARRATOR TWO: Joe, Jr. is working at a desk job with the armed forces in Washington. One day his younger brother Jack pays him a visit.

JOE: Jack! Great to see you. I thought you were in school. What are you doing here?

JACK: Oh, I dunno. Just wanted to see you, I guess.

JOE: Boy, do I envy you.

JACK: You, envy me? You're the one who's Dad's favorite.

JOE: You don't know how difficult that can be. Look at you—Dad lets you do whatever you want. You want to change schools? Go ahead. You want to travel? Sure. Me? All I wanted to do was stay with my unit in England, but because Dad has all these plans for me, I have to stay here where it's safe. And boring.

JACK: At least you're not getting shot at in some dogfight.

JOE: Believe me, little brother, I appreciate it. But every day I get reports about what the Nazis and the Japanese army are up to. They have to be stopped. And here we sit, safe, while others fight.

JACK: Oh, my gosh. That's it! You've given me an idea.

JOE: What is it?

JACK: Mom said that with all our privileges we have a responsibility to help others. That's what I want to do. And what better way than to join the fight for democracy?

JOE: But Jack, you're still in school. And don't forget your back problems.

JACK: Let the army doctors worry about my back. If they say it's good enough for them, then I'm joining up. Will you come with me to the recruiting station?

JOE: Sure. But when Dad hears about it, don't tell him it was me who gave you the idea.

NARRATOR ONE: Jack enlists in the navy and is assigned to the South Pacific, where American forces are fighting the Japanese. Because of his college education, he is a commissioned officer and put in charge of a small torpedo patrol boat—P.T. 109.

★ Scene Three

NARRATOR TWO: The P.T. 109 was not considered a dangerous assignment. But still, they were patrolling in waters well known to the Japanese. Jack, as commander of the boat, was responsible for the small crew.

NARRATOR ONE: It is night patrol on the P.T. 109. Jack, now a lieutenant, is on the bridge with McMahon, one of the crew, when they see a Japanese destroyer bearing down on them.

JACK: Evasive maneuvers! Move! Hard to starboard!

McMAHON: She's too close, Lieutenant!

JACK: Life jackets! All hands!!

NARRATOR TWO: As the crew runs for their life jackets, the Japanese destroyer hits P.T. 109 and cuts it in half. All the crew fall into the water, and some are injured. The P.T. boat sinks. The Japanese destroyer just keeps on going into the dark night.

JACK: Is everyone here?

(The crew counts off. All are accounted for.)

JACK: Okay. Everybody got a life jacket? Anyone injured? McMahon? What about you?

McMAHON: My leg's pretty messed up, Lieutenant.

JACK: Hang on, I'll get you. *(He swims over to McMahon.)*

McMAHON: Save yourself, Lieutenant.

JACK: Pipe down! Hang on to me, and I'll tow you to shore.

McMAHON: But Lieutenant, your back!

JACK: I said, pipe down; we're not leaving anyone behind. Crew, follow me. There are some islands in the distance. Let's swim toward them.

NARRATOR ONE: Jack swam miles to the island with McMahon on his back. Once on the island, he sent distress signals out and the crew was rescued. When he returned home to the United States, he was greeted as a hero. He was awarded the Navy Cross, a medal for extreme bravery. And although his back was more painful than ever because of his life-saving efforts, he started to understand what his mother had meant about serving others.

★ Scene Four

NARRATOR TWO: Jack's success inspired Joe, Jr. to serve in the war effort. Ambassador Kennedy allowed Joe, Jr. to rejoin his unit in Europe.

(The Kennedy family living room. Jack is in his Navy uniform and wearing his Navy Cross. He is with his mother.)

ROSE: Jack, I'm so proud of you.

(As she hugs her son, Ambassador Kennedy enters, looking very upset. Rose runs to him.)

ROSE: Joseph. Joseph! What is it?

AMBASSADOR KENNEDY: Rose, dear, sit down. Prepare yourself. Our beloved son, Joe, Jr. is dead.

ROSE: Oh, no! My boy.

JACK: My brother! How?

AMBASSADOR KENNEDY: Shot down, over Germany. He was supposed to come home after this mission, and he was shot down…my poor son. My Joe.

ROSE: All your dreams for him.

AMBASSADOR KENNEDY: Gone. All gone. What a tragedy!

JACK: Mom, Dad… nothing can bring Joe, Jr. back. But maybe I can do something to help.

AMBASSADOR KENNEDY: You?

ROSE: Son, do you realize what you're saying? Of course, the choice is yours…

AMBASSADOR KENNEDY: Son, you've grown to be a man, you've saved men's lives, and you're a decorated war hero. I cannot tell you what to do. But I can ask. Joe, Jr. was a leader. Now the leader is fallen, and we need a new leader to take his place. Will you do it?

JACK: Of course, dad. Anything you want. I'll do it in honor of my brother Joe.

NARRATOR TWO: It was 1945 when Joe, Jr. died. While World War II came to an end, the Kennedy family mourned. But in 1946, Jack picked up where Joe, Jr. left off. He ran for Congress and was elected to the House of Representatives. His political career had begun.

NARRATOR ONE: Jack never forgot his mother's words about responsibility. When he became president in 1961, he founded the Peace Corps, which gives Americans a chance to serve others overseas in developing nations. He also started the Food Stamp program, which helps low-income families buy quality food.

NARRATOR TWO: In John F. Kennedy's inaugural address, he invited all Americans to "ask not what your country can do for you—ask what you can do for your country." He was urging us to take responsibility for each other. It was a lesson, he said, he had learned from his greatest teacher: his family.

John F. Kennedy
Teacher's Guide

Biography

John F. Kennedy was born on May 29, 1917, in Brookline, Massachusetts. As a young man, he was frail and sick often with a disease called Addison's Disease that left him tired and weak all the time. His family, active in sports and very competitive, tried to combat this through physical activity.

Kennedy idolized his brother, Joe, and was devastated when Joe was killed in World War II. Kennedy himself fought in World War II, commanding the P.T. 109 and saving the crew when the boat was cut in half by a Japanese destroyer.

Kennedy was elected to Congress in 1946 and became a Senator from Massachusetts in 1952. In 1960, he ran for president and, recognizing the power of television in a political campaign, he defeated then–Vice President Nixon in a very close race.

As President, Kennedy established the Peace Corps and the Food Stamp Program. He also guided the nation through the toughest years of the Cold War. He visited Berlin after the Communists had built the Berlin Wall, and stood up to the Soviets when they had installed nuclear missiles in Cuba. While riding in a parade in Dallas, John F. Kennedy was shot three times and died on November 22, 1963. Many of the programs he was working on were finished by his Vice President, Lyndon B. Johnson.

Classroom Activities

★ Talk About It

Like Franklin Delano Roosevelt, John F. Kennedy was born into wealth much greater than the ordinary American will ever possess. And yet, like FDR, Kennedy had great compassion for the economic hardships suffered by poor Americans—and the poor, instead of resenting these rich men, were among their staunchest supporters. Both presidents created programs to help Americans out of poverty (some of which, ironically, are currently criticized for creating more problems than they solved)—Social Security and Food Stamps, to name two.

Students may enjoy speculating about the reasons Kennedy and FDR had such sympathy for the poor of America, and what they would say about their programs today, if they could talk.

★ Write About It

Every American over the age of 40 knows exactly where they were and what they were doing when they heard the news that Kennedy had been shot. Students may be interested in compiling a book or a videotape of interviews of their parents, grandparents, or other older friends and relatives to learn what they were doing and what they thought when they received this news. Encourage students to prepare interview questions in advance. They might call for reflective as well as factual answers, for example: How old were you when Kennedy was shot? Where were you? What were you doing? What do you think the effect on history has been? What do you think Kennedy would be doing today? What would he think of the direction our country has taken?

★ Report on It

John F. Kennedy has been credited with being the first presidential candidate to utilize television in order to gain votes. His debates with Richard M. Nixon, an older, more seasoned public official, are a classic example of how important image is in the television age: Nixon's nervous, rough appearance contrasted badly with Kennedy's handsome polish.

If possible, obtain a videotape or a CD to use with a multimedia computer (they are commercially available and can be borrowed from libraries or from interested parents) and allow students to see the Kennedy-Nixon debate for themselves. Newspaper accounts of the debate can also be accessed from the library. Invite students to evaluate both men's messages and contrast it with their images, and imagine how they themselves would have voted. Encourage them to discuss the issue of image versus substance in American political campaigns.

Alternatively, students may be interested to research social programs, like Food Stamps, the Peace Corps, Medicare and Medicaid, or Project Head Start, that were conceived or promoted by Kennedy and are now being reevaluated.

George Washington • John Adams • Thomas Jefferson • James Madison • James Monroe • John Quincy Adams • Andrew Jackson • Martin Van Buren • William Henry Harrison • John Tyler • James K. Polk • Zachary Taylor • Millard Fillmore • Franklin Pierce • James Buchanan • Abraham Lincoln • Andrew Johnson • Ulysses S. Grant • Rutherford B. Hayes • James A. Garfield • Chester A. Arthur • Grover Cleveland • Benjamin Harrison • Grover Cleveland • William McKinley • Theodore Roosevelt • William H. Taft • Woodrow Wilson • Warren G. Harding • Calvin Coolidge • Herbert C. Hoover • Franklin D. Roosevelt • Harry S Truman • Dwight D. Eisenhower • John F. Kennedy • Lyndon B. Johnson • Richard M. Nixon • Gerald R. Ford • James Earl Carter • Ronald Reagan • George Bush • William Jefferson Clinton

Jimmy Carter
Called To Serve

CAST

NARRATOR ONE

HAMILTON JORDAN

ROSALYNN CARTER

JIMMY CARTER

NARRATOR TWO

PEOPLE ON THE STREET
    (IVAN, VAL, JORGE, MAX)

TV REPORTER

PRESIDENT BILL CLINTON

GENERAL CEDRAS

★ Scene One

NARRATOR ONE: It is November 1980, election night. President Jimmy Carter awaits the election results with his wife, Rosalynn. He has just finished a long and tough campaign against his opponent, Ronald Reagan. Hamilton Jordan, his chief of staff, comes in to give President Carter the results.

JORDAN: The final numbers are in, sir. Ronald Reagan has won the election.

ROSALYNN: Too bad for our country that more people don't appreciate you. Oh, Jimmy, I'm so sorry.

JORDAN: I'm sorry, too, Mr. President.

JIMMY: Well, the people have spoken.

ROSALYNN: Sometimes the people are wrong. After all, you did your best to do great things for this country.

JIMMY: Well, it's Ronald Reagan's turn to try now.

ROSALYNN: Humph! Then it will be the *country* that's sorry.

JIMMY: Now, now, Rosalynn, don't be bitter. Don't forget, there's one job more powerful than being president—that's being a citizen. This isn't the end for me, Rosalynn, it's just the beginning.

JORDAN: Well said, Mr. President.

JIMMY: Thanks, Hamilton. Now, please get Mr. Reagan on the phone, so I can congratulate him on his victory.

★ Scene Two

NARRATOR TWO: It is two years later. Jimmy and Rosalynn Carter have returned to their home in Plains, Georgia. President Ronald Reagan has started implementing his policies. And Jimmy Carter has become a writer of books.

(Jimmy at his desk in Plains. Rosalynn enters.)

JIMMY: Good morning. Rosalynn. Do you remember that man who came to see me yesterday?

ROSALYNN: From that Habitat for Humanity group? Of course. What did he want?

JIMMY: He wanted my help. His group consists of churches and individuals who build houses for the poor. The poor people actually help build the houses, then they move into them.

ROSALYNN: I think it's a great idea to help poor people. How much should we donate?

JIMMY: I wasn't thinking of donating money, exactly. I thought I'd like to go out there and help build some houses. Just think: a former U.S. president with a hard hat on his head and a hammer in his hand, building houses for poor people. It would get Habitat for Humanity on television. And we would be doing a good thing.

ROSALYNN: I don't know, Jimmy. People in Washington have been on the news, saying awful things about you. If you appear in a flannel shirt, building a house …I just don't want to give your detractors any more ammunition to use against you. I don't want you to look foolish.

JIMMY: Rosalynn, I appreciate your concern. But I'm only 58. I'm not done with my life. As a man and a citizen, I still have something to offer the nation. As an ex-president, I command a certain amount of attention. I want to use that attention to do good works and still be a leader.

ROSALYNN: Well…

JIMMY: Rosalynn, I'm going. Are you going with me?

ROSALYNN: Sure. What the heck. It might even be fun.

JIMMY: That's the spirit.

★ Scene Three

NARRATOR: So Jimmy and Rosalynn Carter begin to work for Habitat for Humanity. The news media show pictures on television of Jimmy and Rosalynn swinging hammers and building houses. Many people have opinions about an ex-president doing this kind of work.

IVAN: He just wants to get his face on television.

VAL: We voted him out of office, why can't he just go away?

JORGE: What a fool!

NARRATOR TWO: A few others felt differently.

MAX: Helping the poor is an honorable way of living.

NARRATOR ONE: Jimmy and Rosalynn don't care what anyone says. They enjoy working for Habitat for Humanity, and their presence gets the group attention it would never have otherwise. Donations and volunteers pour in. Many poor people who would have been out on the street have a home thanks to their work.

★ Scene Four
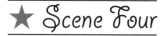

NARRATOR TWO: Meanwhile, Jimmy maintains his interest in foreign affairs—his strength while president.

NARRATOR ONE: He makes several trips overseas at the request of many nations.

NARRATOR TWO: One day a TV reporter stops him and Rosalynn in an airport.

TV REPORTER: Mr. and Mrs. Carter, where are you going?

JIMMY: I have been asked by the government of the Sudan, in Africa, to go over and try to settle their civil war. There are many tribes living there, and they have been fighting with each other. Many, many people have died. So when they asked us for help, we said of course.

TV REPORTER: Why didn't they ask the United States government?

JIMMY: They did, but unfortunately, the people who are currently in the government ignored them. They asked us, and we said we would go.

TV REPORTER: Do you really think you can stop a war in Africa, Mr. Carter?

JIMMY: I don't know, but we have to try.

TV REPORTER: Well, good luck, Mr. Carter.

NARRATOR ONE: Once in the Sudan, Jimmy gets the warring parties to negotiate, and the war ends for a while. People start changing their minds about Jimmy Carter.

JORGE: He was always good in foreign affairs.

MAX: He believes he can solve a problem, and he does.

VAL: Plus, he's very smart. People don't know how smart he is.

NARRATOR TWO: Some, though, remain unconvinced.

SARA: Just looking to get his name in the papers.

IVAN: Besides, who cares about the Sudan, anyway?

NARRATOR ONE: While he was flying back to Georgia, Jimmy meets the same reporter in the airport.

TV REPORTER: Mr. Carter, congratulations on your success in the Sudan.

JIMMY: Thank you.

TV REPORTER: A lot of Americans think that an ex-president shouldn't be getting involved in foreign affairs. How do you answer that?

JIMMY: As you know, I'm a Christian. My religion tells me we are all called upon to be peacemakers. If we act as peacemakers whenever we see any strife, then we are each fulfilling our mission of making the world a better place. Being an ex-president gives me a certain special position. If I can use that position to be a better peacemaker, I will do it. Besides, working for peace anywhere in the world is good for America.

NARRATOR TWO: Jimmy Carter continued to work for peace and human rights. Wherever he went, he was treated with reverence and respect because he had been a President of the United States. But his biggest challenge lies ahead.

★ Scene Five

NARRATOR TWO: In 1994, President Bill Clinton calls former President Carter to the White House.

(The Oval Office. Clinton sits behind the desk. Carter enters. They shake hands.)

JIMMY: Good to see you, Mr. President.

CLINTON: Thanks for coming, Jimmy. I need you for a very important, secret mission. As you know, the people of Haiti elected a president, but then the military leaders threw him out and took over the country again. We have told them that they have to step down, or we will send in the Marines to take the country back. They have refused. Now, Jimmy, Haiti is very unstable right now. I don't want to send in the Marines, but I will if I have to. If I do, many Marines will die, as will many Haitians.

JIMMY: How can I help, Mr. President?

CLINTON: As I said, the military leaders won't step down, but they have agreed to meet with you. I need you to go down there and convince them to move aside. Use your negotiating skills. If you're successful, you could save a lot of lives.

★ Scene Six

NARRATOR: And so, Jimmy Carter leaves for Haiti, a small island nation in the Caribbean. Jimmy takes two other men, Colin Powell and Brent Scowcroft. But when he gets there, the military dictators, led by General Raul Cedras, don't want to negotiate.

(General Cedras's home, from which he runs the government. He sits at a table with Jimmy.)

GENERAL CEDRAS: Your President Clinton does not scare me.

JIMMY: He should. He's got ten divisions of Marines on their way here right now if we can't come to some kind of agreement about turning power over to the democratically elected rulers of this country.

GENERAL CEDRAS: And those Marines will be met by my army if we cannot agree.

JIMMY: With all due respect to you and to your army, General, they're no match for ten United States Marine divisions. So I think we should try to come to an agreement.

GENERAL CEDRAS: You make it sound so easy.

JIMMY: It is easy. If we work at it.

NARRATOR ONE: Jimmy and General Cedras talk into the night. Powell and Scowcroft help, too. But even though they continue to negotiate, they cannot agree.

NARRATOR TWO: Many hours later, with the Marines only a few miles offshore, things look hopeless. Colin Powell enters.

GENERAL CEDRAS: This is getting us nowhere.

POWELL: Mr. Carter, could I speak with you privately?

JIMMY: Excuse me, General. *(He walks off with Powell.)* Yes, Colin?

POWELL: I just got off the phone with Washington. If we do not get to the airport in one hour, the government will not be able to guarantee our safety. We'll be stuck here during the invasion.

JIMMY: You and Brent get ready to leave. Have the car to the airport waiting downstairs. Let me have one more try with the general.

POWELL: I would make it a quick one.

JIMMY: I understand. *(Powell goes off. Jimmy goes back to the General.)* General, our time has run out. In a few minutes my colleagues and I will be off the island, and the Marines will have invaded. I am going to ask you one more time to step down. Please, think of your people.

GENERAL CEDRAS: My people see me as their strong leader.

JIMMY: They won't if you let them be invaded by the U.S. Marines. Then your people will see you as a man who, because of his stubbornness, because of his pride, because he could think of no one but himself, allowed many of their loved ones to be killed. General, think of your people, and how they will feel about you, after you lead them through this time of change—without a shot being fired! You'll be their hero.

GENERAL CEDRAS: Do you think I am an idiot? The moment I step outside, you and your people will arrest me and throw me in jail.

JIMMY: No, we will not. We will ensure that you can go to live in another country safe and sound— as long as you never return to Haiti.

GENERAL CEDRAS: And my family?

JIMMY: They can go with you, of course.

(Powell reenters)

POWELL: Mr. Carter, it's time to leave.

JIMMY: Just one moment…General?

GENERAL CEDRAS: All right, I will go. I will gather my family and go.

JIMMY: Thank you, General.

NARRATOR ONE: Jimmy and Powell give General Cedras the papers to sign, handing power back over to the Haitian president. They then see General Cedras and his family to the airport. When the general and his family get on their plane and fly off, Jimmy and the team come home to the United States.

NARRATOR TWO: This time there are crowds waiting for Jimmy and the team to arrive home. And that same TV reporter asked the people in the crowd what they think of their ex-president.

IVAN: A lot of ex-presidents just go around giving speeches and playing golf, but Carter did good things for others instead.

JORGE: Because he is an ex-president, people around the world respect him. That allows him to get things done.

VAL: What a good man.

MAX: People thought Carter was a loser—but he's become a winner.

SARA: He's my idea of a great American.

NARRATOR TWO: Up until Jimmy Carter, many ex-presidents stayed out of the public eye. They wrote books and occasionally were on TV, but for the most part they faded away and were forgotten.

NARRATOR ONE: Because he was relatively young and energetic, Jimmy Carter had a different view of life after the presidency. Whether it is working for Habitat for Humanity or flying around the world to preserve peace, Jimmy Carter realizes that ex-presidents are very well known, and that fame can be put to good use.

NARRATOR TWO: By not fading away and accepting his defeat, Jimmy Carter today stands as a great American and a great man.

Jimmy Carter
Teacher's Guide

Biography

James Earl ("Jimmy") Carter was born on October 1, 1924, in Plains, Georgia. His father ran a peanut farm. He encouraged Jimmy's interest in the military, and Jimmy entered the United States Naval Academy in 1942. In 1946 he graduated from the Naval Academy and married Rosalynn Smith. Jimmy served in the Navy as an engineer working with nuclear-powered submarines.

He served as a state senator from 1962 to 1966, and in 1970 was elected governor of Georgia. In 1976, he was elected President of the United States, promising a more open government in the wake of the Watergate scandal.

He helped broker the first peace treaty in the Middle East, but the Iranian hostage crisis and a bad domestic economy hurt his popularity. In 1980 he ran for reelection, but did not even have the whole support of his own party, and lost the election to the ultra-popular Ronald Reagan.

Carter was only 58 years old. He went home to Plains, where he wrote books and began working with Habitat for Humanity. His standing as an ex-president helped bring the group fame. His reputation as a top-notch negotiator and a man of peace led to his being asked to monitor elections overseas and help settle international disputes, which he did in the Sudan, in Korea, and in Haiti, where his efforts helped force the junta from power and saved the United States from having to invade under fire. Jimmy lives today with Rosalynn in Plains, Georgia.

Classroom Activities

★ Talk About It

Ask students if they feel ex-presidents should get involved in national affairs. Do they have an expertise that should be called upon to help? Or should they retire and leave the job of governing to the newly elected? List the pros and cons on the board, then discuss with the class if they think having Jimmy Carter work on the international problems he was involved with was a good idea or a bad one. Make sure students support their answers with facts.

Explore with students the idea of negotiation, and trying to convince someone to do something they don't want to do. How was Jimmy Carter effective in this area? Did he use threats? Or did he treat his adversary with respect? Or was it a combination? Use examples from the play of what makes an effective negotiator.

★ Write About It

Have students imagine themselves as the President of the United States. Use an example from current events of a crisis facing the nation, and have the students, as the president, write to former President Carter asking for help. How would they do this without sacrificing their own prestige as president? How would they ask for help if they disagreed with Jimmy Carter politically? Have students use facts from the play and Jimmy Carter's life in their letters.

Working alone or in small groups, ask student to research the Sudan civil war or the Haitian crisis, then have them write a class presentation that explains more fully the role Jimmy Carter played. Students can also work in groups and report on the Camp David accords, Carter's role in the Korean crisis, or the Iranian hostage crisis.

★ Report on It

Being President of the United States is a job. It has requirements, duties, drawbacks, and perks. Some of the details of Jimmy Carter's presidency brings the everyday reality of the job into focus. Students may be interested in learning about the day-to-day job of being President of the United States. Invite those who are interested to call or e-mail the White House to find out more about the job of the presidency, or to do research in the local library to find out what it's like for the people who have held the job that's enabled them to be called "the most powerful person in the world."

Or, have students research the work of Habitat for Humanity, and find a local chapter of the organization, or similar organization, in their community. What kind of work do they do? How are they funded? Have students report to the class about the group, then have them arrange for a group member to come to class and answer questions. Finally, as a class activity, organize a volunteer weekend and have students sign up with their family members, friends, and other classes to help the group. Have students ask the local media to cover their weekend. Explain where the inspiration to do the volunteer work came from—a report on Jimmy Carter.

George Washington • John Adams • Thomas Jefferson • James Madison • James Monroe • John Quincy Adams • Andrew Jackson • Martin Van Buren • William Henry Harrison • John Tyler • James K. Polk • Zachary Taylor • Millard Fillmore • Franklin Pierce • James Buchanan • Abraham Lincoln • Andrew Johnson • Ulysses S. Grant • Rutherford B. Hayes • James A. Garfield • Chester A. Arthur • Grover Cleveland • Benjamin Harrison • Grover Cleveland • William McKinley • Theodore Roosevelt • William H. Taft • Woodrow Wilson • Warren G. Harding • Calvin Coolidge • Herbert C. Hoover • Franklin D. Roosevelt • Harry S Truman • Dwight D. Eisenhower • John F. Kennedy • Lyndon B. Johnson • Richard M. Nixon • Gerald R. Ford • James Earl Carter • Ronald Reagan • George Bush • William Jefferson Clinton

Bill Clinton
Tradition of Greatness

CAST
NARRATOR ONE
NARRATOR TWO
MRS. HUNTER
BILL CLINTON
ROGER CLINTON, SR.
VIRGINIA BLYTHE CLINTON
PRESIDENT JOHN F. KENNEDY

★ Scene One

NARRATOR ONE: In the small town of Hope, Arkansas, William and Virginia Blythe were awaiting the birth of their first child. Mr. Blythe died in an automobile accident three months before the baby, Bill, was born. When Bill was seven, his mother married again, this time to an automobile dealer named Roger Clinton, who became Bill's stepfather. The family moved from Hope to Hot Springs, Arkansas, where Mr. Clinton lived.

NARRATOR TWO: When Bill was sixteen, he started to think about what he wanted to do with his life. His favorite classes were history and civics. He enjoyed learning about the government of the United States, but was unsure if he wanted to make a career out of government service or go into his father's automobile business. He studied hard and listened to the advice of his history teacher, Mrs. Hunter.

MRS. HUNTER: So what the Founding Fathers sought to create was a government in which the people were the ultimate power, not the kings or emperors or the ruling class. This was the difference between what the United States was all about and what the nations of Europe were doing. No nation on earth had ever allowed the people, the ordinary folks, to have such control over their lives.

(The bell rings.)

MRS. HUNTER: Do the questions after chapter twelve for homework tonight.

NARRATOR: While the other students run out of class, Bill lags behind a bit. He slowly packs up his books.

MRS. HUNTER: Bill, do you have a minute?

(Bill walks over to the teacher's desk.)

NARRATOR TWO: Mrs. Hunter hands Bill a piece of paper that makes his eyes pop.

MRS. HUNTER: The American Legion is sponsoring a program called Boys Nation. You have to write an essay about the American government. The boys who write the best essays go to Washington and get to meet President Kennedy.

BILL: President Kennedy? Wow!

MRS. HUNTER: You're the best history student in school, Bill. I think you should represent the school in the essay contest. Does this sound like something you would like to do?

BILL: Does it? You bet!

MRS. HUNTER: Well, you only have a week or so before the essay is due, so you might want to get to work.

BILL: Thank you, Mrs. Hunter. Thanks a lot!

NARRATOR ONE: Bill takes the paper and runs out the door.

★ Scene Two

NARRATOR TWO: Sitting at his kitchen table for hours after school every day that week, Bill works hard on his essay for the Boys Nation competition.

(Roger Clinton, Bill's stepfather, enters. He is wearing his suit from work.)

ROGER: Hey, son, what are you working on?

BILL: It's a contest, Daddy.

ROGER: What kind of contest?

BILL: An essay contest sponsored by the American Legion. The winners get to go to Washington to meet President Kennedy.

ROGER: Huh. And you think *you're* going to win?

BILL: Mrs. Hunter seems to think I can...if I work hard enough.

ROGER: Son, let me tell you something. Life is sometimes full of disappointments. Sometimes you can work as hard as you can and still not get anything to show for it. Now I'm sure some boy is going to go meet President Kennedy, but I don't think it's going to be some car dealer's son. I think they're probably going to find someone else to go down there.

BILL: But, Daddy, I'm working hard, so I think I can—

ROGER: Doesn't matter a lick what you think, son. Listen to me. I know. I know how the world works. Is your mother around?

BILL: She's not back from work yet, Daddy.

ROGER: Well, why don't you come down to the car lot and help me out a little? I could let you work on the new Thunderbirds, introduce you around, you could make a couple of bucks.

BILL: I'd like to, Daddy, but I really have to work on this.

ROGER: I know the real reason you don't want to—it's because you're ashamed of me, isn't it? You're ashamed that your old daddy is just a car salesman, instead of a big-shot, like your idol, President Kennedy.

BILL: No, Daddy, I'm not ashamed—I'm proud of you.

ROGER: Hah! Tell you what—you sit here with your nose in those books and you enter your contest and see if you get to meet President Kennedy. And when they pick some rich man's son to win, just remember I told you so. Then maybe you'll stop dreaming about the White House and the president—and realize your place is down at the car lot...with your old dad! When your Mama comes in, tell her I went out.

(Roger leaves.)

NARRATOR ONE: Although Bill continues to work just as hard, his father's words haunt him. He isn't ashamed of his father, he just knows he doesn't want to sell used cars for a living. What is worse, Roger doesn't seem to value anything Bill works on.

NARRATOR TWO: Bill's mother, however, is different. Virginia Clinton has found work as a nurse in Hot Springs. She goes to the homes of older people and takes care of them. When she returns home from work, she is tired, just like her husband. But she always gives Bill a kiss on the cheek and asks about his schoolwork.

VIRGINIA: Hello, son.

BILL: Hi, Mama.

VIRGINIA: You still working on that Boys Nation essay?

BILL: It's coming along, Mama.

VIRGINIA: Well, when you meet President Kennedy, tell him we here in Hot Springs send our regards. Where's your father?

BILL: He was here a little while ago. He went out.

VIRGINIA: Oh. Well, I have to go get changed. I have a Ladies Auxiliary meeting tonight. Have you eaten?

BILL: Yeah, Mama, I heated up the leftovers you kept for me. Now, I'm just gonna work some more.

VIRGINIA: I'll tell you what. Why don't I skip the meeting and you take a break, and you and your old mama can go down to Hoyers and get ourselves an ice cream?

BILL: Mama, you're not old.

VIRGINIA: Well, son, you're sweet to say that. I'm getting old—but you make me feel young! C'mon, let's go!

★ Scene Three

NARRATOR ONE: Soon, after submitting his essay for the contest, Bill is sitting in Mrs. Hunter's class, when the bell rings.

MRS. HUNTER: Bill, could I see you for a minute?

BILL: Yes, Mrs. Hunter?

MRS. HUNTER: The principal is going to announce the winner of the Boys Nation contest this afternoon, but I wanted to tell you—William Jefferson Clinton—you are going to meet President Kennedy.

BILL: I won? I can't believe it!

(Bill takes the paper from Mrs. Hunter and reads it over.)

BILL: I gotta go home and tell my ma and dad!

MRS. HUNTER: I'll bet they'll both be very proud of you.

BILL: I know my ma will be— and I hope my daddy will.

★ Scene Four

NARRATOR TWO: After school, Bill runs all the way home to tell his mother and Roger about the Boys Nation contest.

NARRATOR ONE: When he gets home, his mother is still at work and Roger is asleep on the sofa. Bill coming in the door wakes him up.

ROGER: What. What! Who's there?

BILL: It's just me, Daddy, Bill. I'm home.

ROGER: Oh.

BILL: Dad? Dad, wake up. Look at this!

ROGER: Huh? What?

BILL: Dad, look. I won the Boys Nation Contest!

ROGER: Huh? You woke me up for that?

BILL: Dad—I'm going to meet President Kennedy!

ROGER: Big deal! I'll tell you what's gonna happen. You're gonna go up there and tell the President of the United States, "Hi, I'm Bill Clinton, and my daddy's a car dealer." And do you know what President John F. Kennedy is going to do?

BILL: (*frowning*) No, Daddy.

ROGER: He's gonna laugh at you. And he has every right to. You're walking around here putting on airs, winning contests—

BILL: I'm not putting on airs, Daddy.

ROGER: Do you think that getting good grades and winning contests is going to help you in life? I bet you didn't know that your Daddy was on the Honor Roll, did you? I sell used cars. People think I cheat them. People laugh at me. That's what good grades get you.

BILL: Daddy, you're wrong. Good grades are important. Sometimes you get good grades, you get to meet President Kennedy.

ROGER: Why is it so important to you to get good grades?

BILL: So you would be proud of me, Daddy. Aren't you proud of me? I knew you got good grades, I want to be just like you. I'm proud of you. Are you proud of me?

NARRATOR TWO: Roger couldn't answer that. He was, in fact, very proud of Bill, and very proud of his good grades.

ROGER: When you go down there and meet the President, what are you gonna say?

BILL: I'm gonna say my dad's the best car dealer in Hot Springs, the best in Arkansas, and the best in the south, that's what I'm gonna say. And that he's a good man.

ROGER: Thank you, Billy. I am proud of you. You've done well. I'm glad you proved me wrong.

★ Scene Five

NARRATOR ONE: Bill travels to Washington with the rest of the Boys Nation winners from the other fifty states. President John F. Kennedy speaks to the boys in the Rose Garden of the White House.

NARRATOR TWO: Bill is with the winners from Arkansas and listens to President Kennedy.

PRESIDENT KENNEDY: This nation, the greatest nation on Earth, is in need of leaders. There is no greater service than service to the nation. And politics, while challenging at times, is the art of that service. On a final note, I can tell you with all sincerity that I would not be surprised if a future president came from this group of good young American men I am speaking to this day.

NARRATOR TWO: President Kennedy then meets with all the boys individually. Bill waits his turn.

(President Kennedy steps down the line of boys. As he reaches Bill, Bill steps forward and shakes President Kennedy's hand.)

PRESIDENT KENNEDY: And what's your name, young man?

BILL: William Jefferson Clinton, sir.

PRESIDENT KENNEDY: Pleasure to meet you, William Clinton.

BILL: It is an honor, Mr. President.

PRESIDENT KENNEDY: How old are you, son?

BILL: Sixteen, sir.

PRESIDENT KENNEDY: And what are you thinking of doing with your life?

BILL: After listening to you today, sir, I think I'd like to be president.

PRESIDENT KENNEDY: I look forward to seeing you in this house someday, William.

NARRATOR ONE: But it is not to be. President Kennedy is killed three months after he meets Bill at Boys Nation. However, Bill never forgets his meeting with the President, nor the goal he told him that day in the Rose Garden.

NARRATOR TWO: Bill continues to do well in school, and he makes his father proud of him. By the time Roger passes away in 1980, he and Bill have become much closer.

NARRATOR: Bill goes on to law school, where he meets his future wife, Hillary Rodham. With her help, he becomes governor of Arkansas. Then, in 1992, he does what he told President Kennedy. He becomes our forty-second president, and returns to the White House, where President Kennedy had inspired him so long ago.

Bill Clinton
Teacher's Guide

Biography

Bill Clinton was born August 19, 1946, in Hope, Arkansas. In 1962, he went to Washington to meet President John Kennedy as part of the Boys Nation program. That meeting inspired Clinton to get into politics. After college he was awarded a Rhodes Scholarship, studying for a year in England. While he was in England, he came out against the War in Vietnam. When he returned he went to Yale Law School to get his law degree. While he was at Yale he met Hillary Rodham, whom he later married. In 1974, she gave up a chance to get into politics herself to move to Little Rock with Bill. Bill was elected Attorney General of Arkansas in 1976, when he was just thirty years old. Two years later, he became the youngest governor in the country when he was elected Governor of Arkansas. He was defeated for reelection in 1982, but won again in 1984 and went on to five straight terms. In 1992 he ran against incumbent President George Bush. He charged Bush with not doing anything about the bad economy in the United States, and with being out of touch with the common man. Clinton won the Presidency from Bush, and on January 21, 1993, became the nation's forty-second President, the first Democrat to hold office since 1980.

Classroom Activities

★ Talk About It

As a young man, Bill Clinton greatly admired President Kennedy. Ask students if there is any government official today whom they look up to and would like to meet. Invite students to talk about why they admire that person. If there is no current political leader they admire, invite them to discuss why that might be, and why ourcurrent political climate makes it difficult for them to look up to public officials.

As an alternative discussion topic, invite students to discuss leaders from history they'd like to meet and tell why.

★ Write About It

Invite students to imitate young Bill Clinton and write their own essay on American government. This may give you an opportunity to review the branches of government, the politcal process or political parties, and other civics topics.

★ Report on It

Invite interested students to write to their local American Legion chapter, the White House, or to the American Newspaper Publishers Association (in Reston, Virginia) to see if they can discover a copy of the actual essay Clinton wrote as a youngster, that won him the trip to Washington. If they are successful, it may be interesting to them to see how the future president thought (and wrote) when he was not much older than they are now.

★ Books for Students

GEORGE WASHINGTON
Osborne, Mary P. *George Washington: leader of a New Nation* (Dial Press, 1991)

JOHN ADAMS
Santrey, Laurence. *John Adams, Brave Patriot* (Troll, 1986)

THOMAS JEFFERSON
Crisman, Ruth. *Thomas Jefferson: Man With a Vision* (Scholastic, 1992)

JOHN QUINCY ADAMS
Harness, Cheryl. *Young John Quincy* (Simon & Schuster, 1994)

ABRAHAM LINCOLN
Sproole, Anna. *Abraham Lincoln: Leader of a Nation in Crisis* (Gareth Stevens, 1992)

THEODORE ROOSEVELT
Weitsman, David. *The Mountain Man and the President* (Raintree Streck, 1992)

WOODROW WILSON
Leavell, Perry. *Woodrow Wilson* (Chelsea House, 1987)

FRANKLIN DELANO ROOSEVELT
Devaney, John. *Franklin Delano Roosevelt, President* (Walker & Co., 1987)

DWIGHT D. EISENHOWER
Sherman, Diane. *The Boy From Abilene: The Story of Dwight D. Eisenhower* (Chelsea House, 1986)

JOHN F. KENNEDY
Levine, I. E. *John Kennedy: Young Man in the White House* (Marshall Cavendish, 1991)

JIMMY CARTER
Wade, Linda R. *James Carter* (Childrens', 1989)

BILL CLINTON
Greene, Carol. *Bill Clinton: 42nd President of the United States* (Childrens', 1995)

★ Books for Teachers

GEORGE WASHINGTON
Cunliffe, Marcus. *George Washington: Man and Monument* (Little, 1958)

Flexner, James Thomas. *George Washington* (Little, 1965–72, 1982)

JOHN ADAMS
Bowen, Catherine Drinker. *John Adams and the American Revolution* (Little, 1950)

Peabody, James Bishop, ed. *John Adams: A Biography in His Own Words* (Newsweek, 1973)

THOMAS JEFFERSON
Brodie, Fawn M. *Thomas Jefferson: An Intimate History* (Norton, 1974)

Malone, Dumas. *Jefferson and His Time* (Little, 1948–81)

JOHN QUINCY ADAMS
Nevins, Allan, ed. *The Diary of John Quincy Adams, 1794–1845* (Ungar, 1969)

Shepherd, Jack. *Cannibals of the Heart: A Personal Biography of Louisa Catherine and John Quincy Adams* (McGraw, 1980)

ABRAHAM LINCOLN
Neely, Mark E., Jr. *The Abraham Lincoln Encyclopedia* (McGraw, 1982)

Oates, Stephen B. *With Malice Toward None: The Life of Abraham Lincoln* (Harper, 1977)

Sandburg, Carl. *Abraham Lincoln: The Prairie Years and The War Years* (Harcourt, 1970)

THEODORE ROOSEVELT
McCullough, David. *Mornings on Horseback* (Simon & Schuster, 1981)

Morris, Edmund. *The Rise of Theodore Roosevelt* (Coward, 1979)

WOODROW WILSON
Bailey, Thomas. *Woodrow Wilson and the Lost Peace. Woodrow Wilson and the Great Betrayal* (Macmillan, 1944–45)

Shachtman, Tom. *Edith and Woodrow: A Presidential Romance* (Putnam, 1981)

FRANKLIN DELANO ROOSEVELT
Freidel, Frank. *Franklin D. Roosevelt* (Little, 1952–73)

Ward, Geoffrey C. *Before the Trumpet: Young Franklin Roosevelt, 1882–1905* (Harper, 1985)

DWIGHT D. EISENHOWER
Ambrose, Stephen. *Eisenhower* (Simon & Schuster, 1983–84)

JOHN F. KENNEDY
Blair, Joan and Blair, Clay, Jr. *The Search for JFK* (Berkley, 1976)

Manchester, William. *Portrait of a President: John F. Kennedy in Profile* (Little, rev., 1967)

JIMMY CARTER
Carter, Jimmy and Carter, Rosalynn. *Everything to Gain: Making the Most of Your Life* (Random, 1987)

Glad, Betty. *Jimmy Carter: In Search of the Great White House* (Norton, 1980)